Practical
Pre-School **Books**

Developing Early
Literacy Skills Outdoors

Look in the shed.

Activity ideas and best practice for teaching and learning outside

by Marianne Sargent

Dedication

This is for Pops and the many hours we spent playing Three Billy Goats Gruff on the bridge in the meadow.

Acknowledgements

Thanks must go to Peter Lambert, Vicki Cawthorn and the children at Chinley Primary School, High Peak, Derbyshire for inviting me in to the reception class to join in with their outdoor activities and allowing the use of a number of photographs.

. . . .

Published by Practical Pre-School Books, A Division of MA Education Ltd, St Jude's Church, Dulwich Road, Herne Hill, London, SE24 0PB.

Tel: 020 7738 5454 www.practicalpreschoolbooks.com

Associate Publisher: Angela Morano Shaw

© MA Education Ltd 2015

Design: Alison Coombes **fonthill**creative 01722 717043

All images © MA Education Ltd. All photos taken by Lucie Carlier, with the exception of the following: p.1 (right) p.13, p.21, p.22 (top left), p.25, p.38, p.46, p.49 (bottom right), p.50, p.56, p.57, p.58, p.60, p.61, p.62, p.65, p.66 and p.74 taken by Marianne Sargent.

ISBN 978-1-909280-85-4

Practical Pre-School Books

Developing Early
Literacy Skills Outdoors

by Marianne Sargent

Contents

Introduction

About the series

This series is intended for early years students and practitioners working with children aged two to five years. It aims to demonstrate how outdoor provision is just as important as the indoor classroom, and highlight the wealth of opportunities that the outdoor environment provides for teaching basic skills and concepts in maths, science and literacy.

In her review of the Early Years Foundation Stage (EYFS) in England, Dame Tickell (2011) recommended a focus on 'how children learn rather than what they learn'. She identified three characteristics of effective learning; playing and exploring, active learning and creating and thinking critically. The books in this series outline the basic concepts

and skills that underpin maths, science and literacy and show how the outdoor environment promotes an active, social and exploratory pedagogical approach to early learning.

Dame Tickell also singled out three 'prime' areas of learning; communication and language, personal, social and emotional development, and physical development. She identified these as fundamentally important for laying secure foundations in preparation for more formal education. Therefore, these books promote early years practice that:

● Involves active practical activities that prompt lively debate and conversation, enabling children to develop the communication and language skills they need to find out about the world and make sense of new information, as well as discuss, extend and evaluate ideas;

- Gives children the chance to practise large and fine motor control, which is not only essential for cognitive development, but important in terms of gaining the strength and coordination needed for future writing and recording;

- Fosters physical and playful activity, promoting healthy personal, social and emotional development by reducing stress, improving mood and boosting motivation and learning.

The books contain a wealth of ideas for enhancing continuous outdoor provision, as well as planning focused maths, science and literacy activities that exploit the unique qualities of the outdoor environment. They also provide advice on planning and assessment, where to find resources and recommendations for further reading. Throughout each book there are links to all four British early years curricula.

Developing Literacy Outdoors

Children develop communication, language and literacy skills through interaction, conversation and play with others. The outdoor environment facilitates active and social play, where children practise speaking and listening to each other and act out roles that involve reading and writing. They do this in an unrestricted space that allows for vocal discussion and argument, which supports their language development and helps them to extend their knowledge and understanding of the world.

Early years pioneer Lev Vygotsky (1986) highlights the relationship between language and learning. It is his contention that language is the key to knowledge and thought. Children develop an understanding of the world by using language to label the things that they see and experience, enabling them to process information, describe and explain its meaning, as well as analyse, question, reason and evaluate. In short, language is what enables children to learn by helping them to take in information, extend their knowledge and form new ideas.

Vygotsky also stresses the importance of social interaction for learning. He advocates a social learning environment where children extend and develop their thinking through discussion with more knowledgeable others. Jerome Bruner (1966) supports this theory and further recommends physical exploration that helps children to develop understanding of basic concepts. He believes that children internalise the knowledge they gain through hands-on social learning experiences, which later leads to more complex abstract thought.

These theories are supported by the hugely influential Researching Effective Pedagogy in the Early Years (REPEY) and Effective Provision of Pre-school Education (EPPE) research projects, which identify the need for good quality verbal interactions that extend and develop thinking. The researchers advocate planning practical experiences for children to 'actively

construct conceptual knowledge' (Siraj-Blatchford et al, 2002) through a balance of taught and 'freely chosen yet potentially instructive child-initiated activities' (Siraj-Blatchford et al, 2004).

All four British early years curricula place much emphasis on the importance of planning hands-on active learning experiences, through which children develop a wide vocabulary that enables them to talk about and describe their observations and experiences.

The outdoor learning environment is the ideal arena for language acquisition and development. Sensory exploration of the natural world not only requires children to tune in and listen, helping them to develop auditory discrimination in preparation for later reading and writing, but it helps them to build a rich vocabulary, enabling them to make connections between the physical world and the language that is used to describe it. Children can draw upon this bank of vocabulary to enrich the language they use when they talk and write.

What's more, when they are outside children are less restricted and have the space to move around and develop the gross and fine motor control they need to be able to hold and control a pencil. There is room to move, dance and become acquainted with the directionality of written English, and there are opportunities to physically play with letters and sounds and make learning about phonics more interesting and interactive.

Laying the Foundations for a successful future

The Effective Pre-school, Primary and Secondary Education (EPPSE 3-16) project report outlines how crucial the REPEY and EPPE research findings are. The report summarises the findings of the entire longitudinal study, which followed nearly 2,600 children from their early years through to the age of 16 and aimed 'to explore the most important influences on developmental pathways that lead to GCSE achievement, mental well-being, social behaviours and aspirations for the future'.

EPPSE reports that children who attended pre-school achieved 'higher total GCSE scores and higher grades in GCSE English and maths'. What's more, attending a high quality setting, where children are exposed to active, social learning experiences, was most beneficial and 'significantly predicted total GCSE scores as well as English and maths grades'. This was also a determining factor in terms of following an academic route into A levels, showing 'that the benefits of pre-school in shaping long term outcomes remain across all phases of schooling and last into young adulthood' (Sylva et al., 2014).

Research shows that spending time outdoors has a positive effect on children's physical development, health, well-being and general learning.

What's more, children can use the natural resources around them to make marks or create scenery and props when re-enacting stories and playing different roles.

The great outdoors

Outdoor provision is a fundamental aspect of early years education and is a statutory requirement across all four early years curricula. The EYFS (DfE, 2014) states that practitioners should provide flexible indoor and outdoor spaces where children can access stimulating resources that promote active exploration and play, while all the time being supported by knowledgeable adults who encourage them to think and ask questions.

The Scottish Curriculum for Excellence (SCE) promotes the outdoors as 'significant' to learning in literacy, numeracy and health and wellbeing, crediting it with helping young children 'make connections experientially, leading to deeper understanding within and between curriculum areas' (LTS, 2010).

The Welsh Foundation Phase Framework (WFPF) sets out the requirement that 'children should as far as possible be able to move freely between the indoors and outdoors' (DCELLS, 2008). Supporting guidance advocates play and 'first-hand experiences' as fundamentally important for the development of language, concentration, concepts and skills 'that will support their future learning' (DCELLS, 2008a). Furthermore, the Northern Ireland Curricular Guidance for

Pre-School Education (NIC) identifies outdoor learning as 'an integral part of the overall educational programme' and promotes a 'planned, purposeful, flexible' approach to teaching and learning where children should be given 'opportunities to explore, experiment, plan and make decisions for themselves' (CCEA, 2006). This is further supported in the Primary Curriculum, which promotes play as the main vehicle for learning in the foundation stage because children best 'develop literacy and numeracy skills in meaningful contexts' (CCEA, 2007).

Learning in the early years is about gaining the fundamental knowledge and skills that provide the basis for future learning. The outdoor environment is an ideal arena for teaching early maths, science and literacy because it offers scope to plan concrete experiences in purposeful contexts, helping children to develop a basic conceptual understanding of these subjects.

About this book

Developing Early Literacy Skills Outdoors considers all aspects of communication, language and literacy including listening and attention, understanding, speaking, reading and writing. It is divided into the following sections:

- Discriminating between sounds

- Becoming aware of sounds in language

- Concentrating and maintaining attention

- Retaining and recalling

- Building a vocabulary

- Understanding

- Developing spoken language

- Expressing thoughts and ideas

- Interacting with others

- Developing a love of stories

- Becoming aware of print

- Developing phonemic awareness

- Linking sounds and letters

- Recognising sight words

- Reading

- Developing pre-writing skills

- Writing.

Each of these aspects is introduced with an explanation of why it is important, together with an overview of the fundamental concepts and skills that underpin it. This is followed up with:

- Ideas for adult-led and adult-initiated outdoor activities that aim to develop children's early knowledge, skills and understanding in communication, language and literacy;

- Suggestions for how to enhance continuous outdoor provision so that it supports child-initiated learning that leads to the development of communication, language and literacy skills;

- General reminders and tips about teaching early communication, language and literacy skills, as well as ideas for how to involve parents;

- The main areas of learning addressed in the English, Scottish, Welsh and Northern Irish early years curriculum frameworks*.

At the end of the book there is advice on planning and organising outdoor learning with suggestions for how to make the most of different sized outside spaces. This is followed by guidance on how to collect evidence of children's learning, with practical tips for observing outdoors and pointers for how to make observation less onerous. Furthermore, there is an example observation sheet together with advice on the effective use of observations to inform assessment and future planning. Finally, there is a list of resource suppliers, as well as links to useful websites and suggestions for further reading.

There is a large body of contemporary research highlighting the benefits of learning outdoors. Helen Bilton (2010) provides a summary:

Physical development

Research highlights links between physical exercise and cognitive development. Exercise increases the ability of blood cells to absorb oxygen and this has a positive knock-on effect for physical brain function.

Health and wellbeing

There is evidence to suggest that spending time outside in the fresh air helps to reduce illness, such as coughs and colds. Furthermore, sunlight activates vitamin D within the body, which is essential for healthy bone growth. Vitamin D can help reduce the chance of cancer and heart disease, which are also linked to sedentary lifestyles. When children are outside they are more active and get more physical exercise, which has health benefits for later life. What's more, exercise reduces stress and improves mood, which in turn boosts motivation and learning.

Learning

Studies highlight the importance of daylight and fresh air for effective learning. Many classrooms have unhealthy levels of carbon dioxide, which impacts upon children's concentration and memory. Children are more able to hear teachers and each other when they are in open spaces, making a quieter outdoor environment more conducive to learning than a noisy classroom. Furthermore, the outdoor environment is more physically challenging and this presents children with opportunities to weigh up physical risk in relation to their own capabilities. Such skills are transferable and applicable to emotional risk, giving children the courage to take on academic and philosophical challenges.

*In the NIC all aspects of communication, language and literacy come under the heading 'language and literacy'. In the SCE they come under 'literacy and English' and in the WFPF they come under 'language, literacy and communication skills'. However, the EYFS separates communication, language and literacy into two areas of learning, the prime area 'communication and language' and the specific area 'literacy'. In addition, the motor skills that children need to be able to write are listed under 'physical development' in the EYFS, NIC and WFPF, and 'health and wellbeing' in the SCE. Therefore, the learning outcomes in this book are selected from all of these areas of learning and indicated in brackets.

The outdoor environment encourages children to engage in social play and practise their speaking and listening skills.

Discriminating between sounds

Listening is the most fundamental literacy skill and this is recognised in the EYFS, where listening and attention are given due prominence within the prime area of learning, communication and language. Listening is an active skill that requires a great deal of effort and practice. Therefore the first four sections of this book primarily focus on developing listening skills.

At the most rudimentary level, listening involves honing in on and sifting out important sounds from background noise. Further to this is the ability to locate where a sound is coming from and distinguish between different sounds. This is otherwise termed as auditory discrimination, a vital skill that aids speech development. Children who have the ability to discriminate between sounds are better able to form clearer sounds in their own speech. What's more, children who can hear and form speech sounds clearly will be better prepared to segment and blend letter sounds when learning to read and write later on.

Auditory discrimination involves the following skills:

- Being able to discriminate between important sounds and background noise

- Being able to distinguish between different sounds

- Being able to locate where a sound is coming from

- Being able to copy or imitate a sound.

The outdoor environment is particularly useful for practising auditory discrimination because of background noise such as other children playing, traffic and weather. What's more, a wide open outdoor space is a great setting for playing listening games that involve locating and identifying different sounds.

Developing Early Literacy Skills Outdoors

Activity 1: What can you hear?

Type of activity: Adult-led, small groups.

Resources: Safe outdoor footpath where the children can concentrate on listening.

What to do: Take the children on a listening walk. Pause every now and then, ask everyone to stand still and listen carefully for different noises and sounds. Choose a child and ask them what they can hear. Ask everyone else to listen out for it too.

Move on, pause and listen again.

Key vocabulary: Listen, sound, noise, loud, quiet, hear.

Extension ideas: Encourage children to discriminate between similar sounds, for example, different types of birds and vehicles.

Go on a listening walk.

HOME LINKS

Ask parents to make their children aware of the sounds around them by drawing their attention to the different things they can hear when out and about in different places.

Activity 3: Hide and seek

Type of activity: Adult-led, small groups.

Resources: Outdoor area with hiding places, range of musical instruments.

What to do: Explain that you are going to play hide and seek with a difference.

Choose a seeker then give all the other children a musical instrument. Explain that they should find hiding places and make noises with their instruments.

Tell the seeker to cover their eyes while the others go and hide. When everyone is hidden away the seeker should use the musical noises to locate the hidden children.

Repeat until everyone has had a turn at being the seeker.

Key vocabulary: Hide, seek, hidden, follow, sound, locate, find, listen, hear, where?

Extension ideas: Ask the hidden children to make it more of a challenge by making their sounds quieter.

Activity 2: Giant sound bingo

Type of activity: Adult-led, small groups of four or six.

Resources: Tarmac floor surface, playground chalks, selection of sound making objects, very large container, twelve beanbags.

What to do: Gather a selection of sound making objects and put them in a very large tub or bin. Use playground chalk to draw out two large lotto boards, each with six boxes featuring pictures that match the selection of sound making objects. Place six beanbags next to each board.

Divide the children into two teams and stand each team next to a board. Explain that you are going to make a sound. They should listen, see if the sound matches a picture on their board and if so, place a beanbag on the picture. The first team to cover all six pictures should shout 'BINGO'.

Keep the sound making objects inside the large container so the children cannot see them as you make each sound.

Key vocabulary: Listen, sound, match, picture, bingo.

Extension ideas: Play bingo using sounds from the local environment, for example, traffic, birds, aeroplanes, roadworks, wind, trains, voices and animals.

Activity 5: Car wash

Type of activity: Adult-led, small groups.

Resources: Hosepipe with different attachments, outside tap, sponges, buckets, washing up liquid.

What to do: Gather the children together and explain that you need some help washing the cars.

Give them sponges and buckets full of soapy water to clean off the dirt. Then give them a hose without any attachments to wash off the soap. Ask the children to describe the sound of the water as it flows out of the hose onto the cars.

Turn the hose off and add a sprinkler attachment. Turn the water back on and ask the children to describe the sound of the water now. Turn the tap to alter the water pressure and ask the children what happens to the sound of the water as it comes out faster or slower.

Change the attachment again and replace it with a spray.

Key vocabulary: Water, wash, sound, listen, trickle, flow, splash, gush, spray, fast, slow, sprinkle, soft, whoosh, tinkle, drip.

Extension ideas: Compare the sound of sponge washing with clear water and soapy water.

Play games that involve listening out for and locating sounds.

Activity 4: Old MacDonald

Type of activity: Adult-led, whole group.

Resources: Large space, preferably with a grassy surface for children to crawl on.

What to do: Gather the children together and sing Old MacDonald, then explain that you are going to play a game. The children should spread out, find a space and listen out for the different animal sounds that you are going to make. Each time you make a sound the children should copy it and move around like the matching animal. For example, a sheep would say 'baa' and munch the grass, a cow would say 'moo' and swish its tail, and a chicken would say 'cluck' and flap its wings.

Key vocabulary: Listen, copy, sound, imitate, moo, baa, cluck, oink, quack, neigh.

Extension ideas: Choose children to come to the front and make the animal noises.

Activity 6: Where did that come from?

Type of activity: Adult-led, small groups.

Resources: Wide open space, identical tambourines or drums.

What to do: Take the children out to a large, wide open space. Give all the children apart from one an identical tambourine or drum and ask them to spread themselves far apart across the space. Ask the child without an instrument to stand at the front with their back to the others.

Move into a position where the child cannot see, then point to one of the other children and ask them to make a noise with their instrument.

The child at the front must listen and judge where the noise came from, then turn and say who it was.

Give everyone a few turns at being the listener.

Key vocabulary: Listen, hear, where, sound, who?

Extension ideas: Make the game more challenging by inviting the child playing the instrument to move from one side of the space to the other. Can the listener point out where the sound moved from and to?

Enhancing continuous provision

Encourage children to use their auditory discrimination skills during independent play by providing resources that prompt them to listen to the environmental sounds that surround them. Provide sensory materials and show the children how to manipulate them to make different sounds. Print off, laminate and display onomatopoeic words to go with each area of provision and read these out as sound effects as the children play (find some examples in the table below). Challenge the children to make up some onomatopoeic words of their own.

Area of provision	Enhancements that encourage children to discriminate between sounds
Water	Glue some glass bottles to a plank of wood and fill each with a different amount of water. Show the children how to blow across the tops to make different sounds. Provide containers of different materials, shapes and sizes for children to explore the varying sound of the water as it is poured and sprinkled between them from different heights. Onomatopoeic words: Splash, splosh, drip, gush, rush, whoosh, slush, ripple, spray, squirt, sprinkle.
Sand	Provide a selection of fine, dry, coarse and wet sand, small and large shells. Supply paper cups, elastic bands, paper, scissors and masking tape for the children to make shakers, and compare the sound that each type of sand/shell makes. Onomatopoeic words: Crunch, scrunch, grit, slop, slap, pat, jangle, rattle.
Construction	Provide sensory building materials that contain sound making objects such as sound prisms or rainbow sound blocks (see resources at the end of the book). Comment on the difference in sound between large and small wooden blocks. Tap on hollow objects and compare them with solid objects. Onomatopoeic words: Thump, thud, crash, smash, bash, batter, clink, clank, crack, scrape, rattle.
Role Play	Outdoor disco: Set up a dance floor with a cordless music player. Put together a compilation that includes songs and music from a variety of genres and in different tempos for the children to listen and dance to. Onomatopoeic words: Boom, beat, shuffle, tap.
Investigation	Provide a range of musical instruments for the children to make different sounds. Hang everyday objects from railings and fences and provide beaters for children to make different sounds. Onomatopoeic words: Bang, knock, beat, boom, tap, crash, clack, twang. Make sounds in nature: Walk through leaves, scrunch up leaves in hands, jump in puddles, stamp on hard ground, step into deep mud, run in the wind. Onomatopoeic words: Swish, rustle, scrunch, splash, stamp, squelch, squidge, gloop, whoosh, whistle.
Physical	Set up a sensory nature trail with different surfaces. Fill large shallow trays with sand, gravel, thick mud, dry straw and water. Allow the children to take off their shoes and walk across and listen to the sounds of the different substances under their feet. Onomatopoeic words: Slurp, squelch, crunch, stamp, whoosh, whirl, flutter, rustle.
Garden	Hang wind chimes made of different materials such as bamboo, metal, shells and beads. Download some birdsong recordings onto an MP3 player and let it play inside a bird hide or tent for the children to listen to and match to bird sounds outside. Find some samples on the BBC Radio 4 website (www.bbc.co.uk/radio4/science/birdsong.shtml). These are all about one minute long with accompanying voiceover. Onomatopoeic words: Tinkle, jangle, jingle, tweet, twit-twoo, coo, cluck.

Curriculum links

Discriminating between sounds covers the following areas of learning and development:

EYFS	Locates a range of sounds with accuracy; recognises and responds to many familiar sounds; focuses attention; frequently imitates sounds and words (CL).
NIC	Identifies environmental sounds; listens with increasing attentiveness and for longer periods of time; develops auditory discrimination and memory (LL).
SCE	Develops an awareness of when to talk and when to listen (LE).
WFPF	Listens and responds appropriately and effectively, with growing attention and concentration (LLC).

Becoming aware of sounds in language

As well as having the ability to discriminate between environmental sounds, children need phonological awareness, or an awareness of sounds in language.

Sue Palmer and Ros Bayley (2013) provide a comprehensive overview of the stages involved in developing phonological awareness and explain how steady beat, rhythm and rhyme play are core to this process. Playing with language and words helps to build children's awareness of syllables, sounds and rhymes. Children who are exposed to rhythmical, rhyming texts and songs with repeated refrains from a young age will have a greater awareness of the sounds, rhythms and patterns of spoken and written language. This basic experience will enable children to hear individual letter sounds as well as letter patterns within words (phonemic awareness), which is essential for blending and segmenting sounds when reading and writing.

Developing phonological awareness involves the following skills and concepts:

- Understanding that language is made up of words

- Understanding that some words can be broken up into chunks or syllables

- Being able to identify, copy and continue a rhyming string

- Being able to identify, copy and compose an alliterative phrase.

Steady beat, rhythm and rhyme go hand-in-hand with physical movement and dance. Take advantage of outdoor space to get children playing literacy games, singing songs and acting out rhymes.

Activity 1: Nature beats

Type of activity: Adult-led, small groups.

Resources: Natural outdoor environment.

What to do: Take the children on a walk and ask them to point out any natural objects that they spot along the way.

Each time a child points something out, pause, say the word and clap or jump the syllables. For example, con-ker, leaf, syc-a-more, grass, dais-y, dand-e-lion, pot-a-to.

Key vocabulary: Names of natural objects.

Extension ideas: Change the focus to vehicles, for example, car, lor-ry, di-gger, bus, tax-i, ae-ro-plane. Challenge the children to spot objects with a certain number of syllables.

Activity 3: Outdoor rap

Type of activity: Adult-initiated, during independent play.

Resources: Notepad and pen.

What to do: Gather a few children and recite the following rap:

Stuck inside with nothing to do?
Open the door to a world that's new.
Come wind or snow or rain or sun,
Grab your shoes and have some fun.

Bugs and mud and sticks and grass,
Racing, chasing, throw and pass.
By yourself or with your friends,
The fun outside never ends.

Take the children outside and repeat the rap. This time clap and move to the beat. Use the surrounding environment to continue the rap. Make up a couple of lines, start another then pause and invite the children to continue. Help them keep to the beat and think of rhyming words. Write their ideas down to share with other children later.

Key vocabulary: Rap, beat, rhyme, word, rhythm.

Extension ideas: Find more ideas for active rapping activities in *Ros Bayley's Action Raps*, published by Lawrence Educational (www.lawrenceeducational.co.uk).

Activity 2: We're Going on a Bear Hunt

Type of activity: Adult-led, small groups.

Resources: Garden or woodland area with grass, sticks, leaves, flowers, bark, wood, pinecones, mud.

What to do: Read *We're Going on a Bear Hunt* by Michael Rosen and Helen Oxenbury to the children. Show the children Michael Rosen's performance of the Bear Hunt song on the internet (www.jointhebearhunt.com).

Go outside to a garden or visit a nearby woodland area, divide the children into small groups and challenge them to create the scenes of the story using natural materials. When they have finished get them to recite Michael Rosen's song, emphasising key phrases, words and sounds.

Key vocabulary: Wavy, swishy, swashy, splash, splosh, oozy, squelch, squerch, stumble, trip, whirling, hoooo woooo, tiptoe.

Extension ideas: Encourage the children to think of onomatopoeic words of their own to describe how the different terrains feel, look and sound.

Create a bear hunt scene and recite Michael Rosen's song.

Sing some traditional circle game songs.

Activity 4: Funny phrases

Type of activity: Adult-initiated, during independent play.

Resources: Small world fantasy or superhero characters.

What to do: Set up a fantasy or superhero small world scenario in the outdoor area.

Join the children as they play, ask them to name the different characters and make up a funny or nonsense alliterative phrase to match the initial sound of each character's name. For example, Silly Spiderman got stuck in some sticky slime, or Bonkers Batman has baskets bursting with bunnies, or Flower fairies are full of fabulous fun.

Challenge the children to make up their own alliterative phrases.

Key vocabulary: Alliteration, first, initial, sound, same, repeat, funny, phrase.

Extension ideas: Challenge the children to make up alliterative superhero names based around the initial sound in their own names, for example, Lauren Laser-eyes, Geronimo George or Fire-force Finn.

Activity 5: Hokey Cokey

Type of activity: Adult-led, whole group.

Resources: Selection of traditional circle game songs.

What to do: Take the children out to a big open space to play the following circle singing games:

- The Hokey Cokey
- Looby Loo
- Here we go round the mulberry bush
- This old man
- Oranges and lemons
- The farmer's in his den

Find the lyrics to these songs, as well as samples of the tunes on The Nursery Rhymes Collections website (http://nurseryrhymescollections.com). The actions for most of these games can be found in *The Little Book of Playground Games* by Simon MacDonald, published by Featherstone (www.bloomsbury.com).

Key vocabulary: Sing, rhyme, action, circle, dance, beat, rhythm.

Extension ideas: Set up a wireless CD or MP3 player outside and leave a CD of circle game songs playing for the children to play independently.

Activity 6: Rhyming roulette

Type of activity: Adult-led, small groups.

Resources: Large umbrella, laminated rhyming words (use pictures to make the game easier), sticky-backed Velcro.

What to do: Use sticky-backed Velcro to fix a selection of short, laminated words inside an open umbrella. Give each child a card with a word that rhymes with one of the words on the umbrella. Read out the children's words and ask each child to repeat their word.

Hold the open umbrella upside-down, its point to the floor. Twirl it and let go. When the umbrella stops, read out the word that is resting on the ground. Then ask the children: 'Who is holding the word that rhymes?'

Key vocabulary: Rhyme, sound, same, match.

Extension ideas: Encourage the children to continue the rhyming string by suggesting more words. Make this game easier by using picture cards that feature rhyming objects.

HOME LINKS

Send home a booklet of outdoor action rhymes that parents can sing with their children when they are out and about.

Enhancing continuous provision

As well as playing games, a most effective way of helping children become aware of sounds in language is by exposing them to as many different rhythmical and rhyming texts as possible. Do this outside as well as inside by carefully selecting books and placing them around and about outdoor activities and resources. Print out the lyrics from songs and rhymes and display them on the inside of windows facing out, or inside playhouses, sheds and shelters. Select rhymes that tie in with current projects and themes and display them alongside resources and equipment.

Invite the children to share the stories, listen to rhymes and make up their own. Introduce rhyming strings and see if they can continue them. Find examples in the table below:

Area of provision	Enhancements that help children to become aware of sounds in language
Water	Place copies of *A Commotion in the Ocean* by Giles Andreae and David Wojtowycz and *Tiddler* by Julia Donaldson and Axel Scheffler near the water tray. Fill the tray with toy fish and exotic toy sea creatures together with fishing boats and netting. Rhyming strings: Splash, dash, crash… Drip, slip, trip… Slush, gush, rush…
Sand	Select some poems from a collection such as *Seaside Poems* by Jill Bennet and Nick Sharratt. Enlarge, print and display them near the sandpit. Transform the sandpit and surrounding area into a seaside scene with buckets and spades, inflatables, deckchairs, picnic blankets, mermaids and toy sea creatures. Invite the children to bring in their own seaside photos to display alongside the poems. Rhyming strings: Sand, hand, tanned… Dig, big, rig… Sun, run, fun…
Construction	Place copies of *Tough Trucks and Dazzling Diggers* by Tony Mitton and Ant Parker next to a small world building site with real gravel, stones and sand. Rhyming strings: Tip, rip, dip… Block, rock, knock… Fill, drill, hill…
Role Play	Set out a picnic blanket with a large basket containing plastic strawberries, apples and pears. Provide cuddly toys including a rabbit, squirrel, mouse, goose, duck and chicken with a copy of *We're Going on a Picnic!* by Pat Hutchins. Rhyming strings: Feed, greed, lead… Berry, cherry, merry… Lunch, munch, crunch…
Investigation	Provide a range of percussion instruments including drums, tambourines, cymbals, triangles, maracas, castanets and wooden blocks for the children to play out rhythms and beats as they recite their own songs and rhymes. Rhyming strings: Bang, twang, sang… Hit, sit, pit… Tap, rap, cap…
Physical	Enlarge, print and laminate a selection of traditional songs that encourage children to march and move to a steady beat, such as The Grand Old Duke of York, If you're happy and you know it, Heads, shoulders, knees and toes, Jelly on a plate and One finger, one thumb, keep moving. Sing the songs to the children and encourage them to move in time.
Garden	Enlarge, print and laminate a selection of poems from Shirley Hughes' *Olly and Me Out and About*. Hang the poems on trees and fences around the garden area. Read them to the children. Provide digital cameras for the children to take photos of each other enjoying the natural elements. Rhyming strings: Mud, thud, crud… Wet, set, bet… Sky, dry, sigh…

Curriculum links

Becoming aware of sounds in language covers the following areas of learning and development:

EYFS	Listens to and enjoys rhythmic patterns in rhymes and stories; shows interest in play with sounds, songs and rhymes (CL). Enjoys rhyming and rhythmic activities; shows awareness of rhyme and alliteration; recognises rhythm in spoken words; continues a rhyming string (L).
NIC	Repeats familiar phrases/sound sequences; responds to a steady beat; identifies syllables; identifies and generates rhymes; develops auditory discrimination and memory; understands that words are made up of sounds and syllables; listens to a wide range of stories, poems, songs and music (LL).
SCE	Enjoys exploring and playing with the patterns of sounds and language and can use what they learn (LE).
WFPF	Develops phonological knowledge; experiences a range of stimuli including, simple rhymes, nursery rhymes, songs, stories and poetry; understands that there is variety in the language that they hear around them (LLC).

Concentrating and maintaining attention

Effective listening involves concentrating and maintaining attention. Children who learn these skills early on will go on to be more successful learners because they will have the ability to take in and retain useful and important information. What's more, they will be able to focus on and complete tasks more quickly, making learning more enjoyable and reducing the chance that it will feel like a chore. Therefore, in the early years it is a good idea to play plenty of games that give children practice at focusing and concentrating. This can be done through activities that involve listening for cues and instructions, as well as through games that ask the children to look closely and pay attention to detail.

Concentrating and maintaining attention involves the following skills:

● Being able to sit/stand still and maintain eye contact

● Being able to ignore distractions

● Being able to respond to aural and visual cues

● Being able to focus

● Being able to pay attention to detail.

The outdoor environment is great for practising these skills. First, because there are so many distractions that need to be tuned out, and second, because there is enough space to play fun active games that encourage the children to pay attention and focus on the task at hand. What's more, there is also scope for quieter activities that involve sitting still and listening.

Activity 1: Roll the ball

Type of activity: Adult-led, any sized groups.

Resources: Large ball.

What to do: Instruct the children to hold hands, form a large circle and drop their hands. Explain that you are going to say a name and roll the ball to that particular child. The child must catch the ball, then say another child's name and roll the ball to them. And so on.

Key vocabulary: Listen, name, roll, catch.

Extension ideas: Adapt the game by throwing or bouncing the ball, or play without a ball and get the children to swap places instead. Extend the game by asking children to say who they are rolling the ball to and who that person should roll to next.

Play games that encourage children to concentrate.

HOME LINKS

Compile a booklet of outdoor games that parents can play with their children to help them improve their focus and concentration.

Activity 3: Wait for it...

Type of activity: Adult-led, small groups.

Resources: Picnic blanket, pre-written traditional tales.

What to do: Prepare for this activity by choosing some traditional tales and writing them out. Choose a particular word or phrase that can be repeated throughout each story, for example the names Goldilocks, Jack or Wolf, and the phrases, 'trip trapping' or 'huff and puff'. Ensure that these words and phrases are repeated frequently and highlight them for your own reference.

When out and about take time out to tell a story. Explain that you are going to see how well the children can listen. Give them a word or phrase to listen out for and a signal that they should do every time they hear it, for example thumbs up or hands on heads.

Key vocabulary: Listen carefully, hear, word, phrase.

Extension ideas: Turn this into an active game. Move into a large space, spread out and sit down. Sing a song or rhyme that has repeated refrains. Every time the children hear a certain word or phrase they should jump up to their feet.

Activity 2: Seek it out

Type of activity: Adult-led, groups of three.

Resources: Small object such as a ball or toy car.

What to do: Take a small group of children outside when it is quiet. Show them a small object and explain that you are going to hide it somewhere. The children should turn around to face a wall and cover their eyes. They should then listen very carefully as you describe where you are going and where you are hiding the object. When the object is hidden the children should turn around and look for the object. Those children who were listening carefully will know where to look.

Key vocabulary: Listen carefully, hear, direction, describe, description, hide, hidden, location, find.

Extension ideas: Invite the children to take your place and have a go at hiding the object.

Listen out for particular words and phrases in stories.

Play listening action games.

Activity 4: Popping corn

Type of activity: Adult-led, whole group.

Resources: Wide open space, whistle.

What to do: Take the children out to a large space and instruct them to spread out. Explain that they are going to pretend to be popping kernels of corn. Begin with a quiet voice and gradually increase the volume as you describe the cooker being turned on, the heat firing up, the pan warming up, the kernels beginning to rattle, then expanding and expanding until…. POP, POP, POP, POP, POP! Demonstrate to the children how they should begin crouched down and curled up very small, then slowly begin to shake and make themselves bigger, forming a round shape with their arms that keeps expanding until they hear the word 'POP' when they should explode and jump around all over the place. When the whistle blows they should curl back up ready to start again.

Key vocabulary: Popcorn, kernel, expand, pop, listen.

Extension ideas: Play more games that involve listening and performing actions, such as Jack in the Box, Runner Beans or Simon Says.

Activity 5: Guess who?

Type of activity: Adult-led, whole group.

Resources: Very large blanket, whistle.

What to do: Take the children to a wide open space. Explain that when you blow the whistle they should run around, then when you blow it again they should stop, crouch down into a ball on the floor and cover their eyes. Emphasise the importance of no peeping!

When the children are all crouched down tell them you are going to lay a blanket over one child, who must not make a sound. When you have done that ask all the other children to stand up and gather around.

The children must ask the child under the blanket some questions to help figure out who it is. They will either guess through hearing the hidden child's voice or through what the child reveals in their answers. (Obviously they are not allowed to ask the child to tell them their name!)

Key vocabulary: Pay attention, missing, who?

Extension ideas: Leave out the questioning part so the children have to deduce who is under the blanket by looking around at each other to see who is missing.

Activity 6: Traffic lights

Type of activity: Adult-led, whole group.

Resources: Wide open space, table tennis bats, red, orange and green paper, double-sided sticky tape, scissors.

What to do: Cover some table tennis bats in green, orange and red paper. Take the children out to a large space and instruct them to spread out. Explain that when you hold up the colour red and shout 'red' the children should stop, when you hold up the colour orange and shout 'orange' the children should walk around, and when you hold up the colour green and shout 'green' the children should run. Take some time to decide which direction everyone will be travelling in before you start to avoid collisions during the game. After playing the game for a while choose volunteers to come to the front and be the caller.

Key vocabulary: Red, orange, green, stop, walk, run, listen.

Extension ideas: Stop using the visual cues so the children have to rely solely on listening.

Enhancing continuous provision

Throughout the day it is a good idea to use sounds as cues for particular routines or tasks. This encourages children to listen out for certain signals that require a response. For example, try using a tambourine or bells to give everyone notice that it will be tidy-up time in five minutes. Set up a stereo that can be heard both indoors and outside and play a tidy-up sound track for the children to sing along to as they clear everything away. When the track finishes this is a signal that the children should go inside to the carpet area and sit down. Another idea is to clap a repetitive rhythm when you want to get everyone's attention. Do this next to a group of children and wait for them to join in. Before long everyone will be looking at you and clapping in time.

Set up activities that require children to concentrate, focus and maintain attention. Once the children have been shown how to play each of the games in the table below they will happily play them independently.

Area of provision	Enhancements that help children to concentrate and maintain attention
Water	Set up a fishing game. Drop some magnetic fish into the water and provide magnetic fishing rods. Give the children certain aims that will require them to concentrate, for instance, catch numbered fish in numerical order or catch and sort the fish according to colour or pattern.
Sand	Set up a site of palaeontological interest. Bury some dinosaur bones and fossils in the sand tray or pit and supply small brushes and tools for the children to excavate with. Encourage them to take their time and brush away the sand with care. Give them digital cameras to photograph their finds. Provide pictures of dinosaurs and fossilised skeletons for the children to look closely at different details and compare with their finds.
Construction	Set up a spot the difference game. Use colourful bricks to build small constructions, make pictures or create patterns in pairs with slight differences. Challenge the children to spot the difference then create some of their own to challenge their friends. Use crates to create a large scale maze. Challenge the children to alter it and create new routes and dead ends.
Role Play	CBeebies Story time: Draw or print a picture of the CBeebies story time logo and display it in a comfy spot with a blanket and cushions. Provide a selection of familiar and popular picture books. Remember to include books with detailed illustrations that encourage children to look for little details such as *Once Upon a Time* by John Prater and *The Little Red Train* books by Benedict Blathwayt.
Investigation	Set up a cups game. Place three opaque cups on a table with a basket of conkers, acorns or pinecones. Show the children how to play cups, where you place an object under one cup then swap them around several times while the audience watches and tries to keep track of the object. Use playground chalks to draw 3 x 3 grids on the floor for the children to play noughts and crosses.
Physical	Set up a wireless CD or MP3 player that the children can use to play listen and respond games such as musical statues, musical bumps or sleeping lions.
Garden	Create quiet conversation corners where the children can sit quietly and talk to each other. Use pop up tents, cordon off areas with barriers and build dens. Laminate and hang 'I Spy' cards around the outdoor area. Print pictures of flowers, birds, minibeasts and natural items with a small 'I Spy' logo in the corner to encourage children to use their observation skills to find examples of each.

Curriculum links

Concentrating and maintaining attention covers the following areas of learning and development:

EYFS	Focuses attention; maintains attention, concentrates and sits quietly during appropriate activity; can listen attentively in a range of situations (CL). Listens to stories with increasing attention and recall (L).
NIC	Develops auditory and visual discrimination and memory; listens with increasing attentiveness and for longer periods of time (LL).
SCE	When listening and talking in different situations, is learning to take turns and is developing awareness of when to talk and when to listen; listens and watches for useful or interesting information and uses this to make choices or learn new things (LE).
WFPF	Views and listens carefully to a variety of visual stimuli; listens and responds appropriately and effectively, with growing attention and concentration (LLC).

Retaining and recalling

Once children have the ability to concentrate and maintain attention they will be better able to retain and recall information, or in other words, commit information to memory. Short-term memory, sometimes referred to as working memory, is needed for functioning from moment to moment during everyday life. Long-term memory is a permanent store that is drawn upon for information about past experiences and events, as well as everyday general knowledge and facts about how the world works. Children who have the ability to listen, together with a well-developed memory, will be more adept at learning across all subject areas.

Retaining and recalling involves the following skills:

- Being able to focus, concentrate and maintain attention

- Being able to pay attention to detail

- Being able to identify what is important

- Being able to make links and recall relevant information from memory.

Memory is affected by feeling and emotion. If children are disinterested or stressed their memory will not function properly, and this will impact upon the amount of information that they are able to retain and recall. Therefore, in order to help children improve their memory, it is important to plan fun and entertaining learning experiences that grab their attention and make them want to join in. Play fun games that require them to use their short-term memory and use popular songs, rhymes and stories to help them commit information to their long-term memory.

Activity 1: Mimicking moves

Type of activity: Adult-led, groups of up to six.

Resources: Open outdoor space.

What to do: Instruct the children to make a circle by holding hands and moving apart until their arms are outstretched, then dropping their hands to their sides so they have a good amount of space either side of them.

Explain that you are going to play a movement memory game whereby the children have to copy each other's movements.

Begin by making a single movement, for example a jump, then turn to the child next to you and explain that they should do the jump and another move of their own. The next child should copy these two moves and add another move of their own and so on.

Key vocabulary: Pay attention, watch, copy, remember, sequence, memory.

Extension ideas: Instead of asking the children to build the sequence by adding another move on their turn, simplify the game by passing one move around the circle, then passing two moves around, then three, and so on. Play the game with musical instruments and get the children to play sound sequences instead.

Activity 3: The Very Hungry Caterpillar

Type of activity: Adult-led, small groups.

Resources: Small and large toy caterpillars, toy butterfly, brown paper bag (moulded into the shape of a cocoon), large leaf, dried bean (use as an egg), apple, two pears, three plums, four strawberries, five oranges, piece of cake, ice-cream cone, pickle, cheese, salami, lollipop, cherry pie, sausage, cupcake and watermelon (real, toy or pictures).

What to do: Take the children out to the garden area and read *The Very Hungry Caterpillar* by Eric Carle. Use the above resources to retell the story.

Key vocabulary: Story, listen, remember, sequence, what happens next?

Extension ideas: Use the props to play sequencing games and get the children to spot what's missing.

Activity 2: A Squash and a Squeeze

Type of activity: Adult-led, small groups.

Resources: Very large cardboard box, strong thick masking tape, brown, grey, red and green poster paint, large and small paintbrushes, black marker pen, PVA glue, scissors or sharp knife, cuddly toy cow, goat, pig and chicken.

What to do: Before starting this activity use a very large cardboard box to make a house that at least two children can fit inside. Cut the flaps off the bottom of the box, open up the flaps on the top and tape them into a roof shape; cut out a window and paint on some green shutters; cut a door opening, fold the card back so it opens and closes and paint it brown; paint the roof red and the walls grey. Let the paint dry then use a black marker pen to outline details. Paint the entire box in watered down PVA glue to make it damp-proof and more durable.

Bring the children together to read *A Squash and a Squeeze* by Julia Donaldson and Axel Scheffler. Take them out to the house and re-enact the story using cuddly toy animals.

Key vocabulary: Story, listen, remember, sequence, which animal? what happens next?

Extension ideas: Leave the house, animals and book out for the children to re-enact the story independently. Keep this house and reuse it for re-enacting other stories such as Goldilocks and the Three Bears, The Three Little Pigs, *One Snowy Night* by Nick Butterworth or *The Doorbell Rang* by Pat Hutchins.

Can the children spot what is missing?

Play an outdoor version of Matching Pairs.

Activity 4: Matching pairs

Type of activity: Adult-led, small groups.

Resources: 20 plant pots, 10 matching pairs of natural items.

What to do: Neatly set out 20 plant pots upside down in four rows of five on the floor in the outdoor area. Collect 10 matching pairs of natural items, for example two conkers, two sycamore seeds, two pebbles, two pinecones, etc. Place an object under each plant pot.

Bring the children over to play this game two at a time or in small teams. The aim of the game is to choose a plant pot, look underneath it to see what is there and then find the other plant pot with a matching object. Each time a child/team gets a matching pair they get to keep the pots and contents. If they turn over two items that do not match they must turn them back over and leave them there. At the end of the game the team that has collected the most matching pairs wins.

Key vocabulary: Remember, look, where, match, memory.

Extension ideas: Increase or decrease the number of plant pots to make the game more or less of a challenge. Leave the game set out for the children to play independently.

Activity 5: Memorable walk

Type of activity: Adult-led, small groups.

Resources: Safe outdoor footpath where the children can look around as they walk, variety of objects.

What to do: Plan a route for an outdoor walk. Along the route place a variety of objects in unusual places, for example, a wellington boot up a tree, a teddy bear sitting with a sandwich on a patch of grass, a large toy dinosaur in a puddle, a frying pan hanging on a gate and a large toy fire engine on a low roof.

Gather the children and explain that you are going to take them on a walk and you would like them to pay attention to what they see around them because at the end you are going to ask them what they saw. At the end of the walk see how many items the children can remember seeing and where they were.

Key vocabulary: Pay attention, look, see, what, where, remember, memory.

Extension ideas: Go on nature walks and ask the children to try and remember everyday natural items that are less memorable.

HOME LINKS

Ask parents to help their children make a diary featuring photos of things they did over the weekend. Help the children use their weekend diaries to recall what they did and tell others in the setting.

Don't forget to think about...

...using traditional tales and rhymes to help children improve their memories through repetition. Plan regular story and rhyme times into the day and ensure these take place both indoors and outside.

Put things in unusual places and see if the children can remember where they saw them.

Developing Early Literacy Skills Outdoors

Enhancing continuous provision

Use stories, rhymes and games to enhance the continuous outdoor provision so that children are encouraged to use their memories as they play independently. Many children will be familiar with a range of traditional tales, which lend themselves well to retelling and re-enacting. Source clear and simple picture books, such as the *Flip-up Fairy Tales*, published by Child's Play or the *Ladybird First Favourite Tales* and leave these in the different areas of learning along with props that the children can use to act out the stories. Set up a washing line with a basket of laminated story sequencing cards featuring well-known stories. Laminate nursery rhymes and action songs and leave them around to inspire children to sing them as they play.

Area of provision	Enhancements that encourage children to retain and recall
Water	Set up a watery version of the tray game. Float a large boat in the tray and provide a tub of small objects such as toy sea creatures, sailors, shells, pebbles and corks. Place a selection of objects on the boat, let the children study it for a few minutes, cover the boat with an opaque carrier bag and remove an object. Reveal the boat and ask the children to guess what is missing.
Sand	Leave a beach bag with a range of seaside toys and equipment including a beach ball, bucket, spade, towel, swimsuit, sunglasses and sunhat. Use playground chalk to write on the floor next to the sand pit or tray, 'I went to the seaside and I took…' Encourage the children to use the props to play this memory game.
Construction	Provide small construction straw bales, mini life-size bricks and sticks (big enough for den building) along with a copy of The Three Little Pigs for the children to build the houses and act out the story. Provide building blocks, a copy of Three Billy Goats Gruff and some puppets. Provide building blocks, a laminated copy of Humpty Dumpty and a big Humpty Dumpty toy.
Role Play	The Enormous Turnip: Half bury a large turnip in a soil patch and supply some dressing up clothes for the children to take the roles of the old man, old woman, neighbour and son. Provide some masks to represent the cat and dog. Place a large cooking pot, bowls and utensils nearby for the turnip soup. Laminate some numbered story cards to help the children retell this traditional tale in sequence.
Investigation	Set up a table and lay out a series of objects that feel very different to the touch, for example a conker, a pinecone, a pebble, a twig and a leaf. Provide a blindfold. Explain that the aim of the game is for a blindfolded child to touch the items in sequence before they are mixed up. They should then remove the blindfold and attempt to remember the sequence and put the items back as they were.
Physical	We're Going on a Bear Hunt: Lay a couple of mats on the floor, set up a high bar to crawl under, a low bar to step over and a tunnel to crawl through. Write on the floor in playground chalk: We can't go over it, we can't go under it, we have to go through it!
Garden	Print, laminate and leave out illustrated versions of the following outdoor rhymes: Two little dicky birds, There's a worm at the bottom of my garden, Incy wincy spider, If you go down to the woods today, Rain, rain, go away and The sun has got his hat on.

Curriculum links

Retaining and recalling covers the following areas of learning and development:

EYFS	Maintains attention, concentrates and sits quietly during appropriate activity; joins in with repeated refrains and anticipates key events and phrases in rhymes and stories (CL). Listens to and joins in with stories and poems, one-to-one and in small groups (L); listens to stories with increasing attention and recall (L).
NIC	Develops auditory and visual discrimination and memory; listens to a wide range of stories, poems, songs and music; repeats familiar phrases; recalls sequence and detail; listens with increasing attentiveness and for longer periods of time (LL).
SCE	When listening and talking in different situations, is learning to take turns and is developing awareness of when to talk and when to listen; listens and watches for useful or interesting information and uses this to make choices or learn new things; enjoys exploring and choosing stories and other texts to watch, read or listen to (LE).
WFPF	Listens and responds appropriately and effectively, with growing attention and concentration; repeats rhymes and poems, sometimes from memory; tells and retells stories, both real and imagined (LLC).

Building a vocabulary

A good vocabulary has implications for progression in all areas of learning. Children who have the words to explain their needs and wants will be happier and less frustrated than those who cannot verbalise how they are feeling. They will progress further in maths, science and humanities because they will have the language they need to label, process information, explain, describe and reason. What's more, a good vocabulary is of course invaluable for the creative arts and English because it allows children to transcribe the contents of their imaginations into spoken and written language.

Building a vocabulary involves the following skills and concepts:

- Understanding that language conveys meaning

- Understanding and being able to use a variety of nouns and verbs to name and describe

- Understanding and being able to use a variety of adjectives and adverbs to describe

- Being able to describe position and sequence

- Being able to classify and categorise.

The outdoor environment is a rich source of stimuli that begs to be experienced and described. Everywhere you turn there are natural and man-made phenomena that appeal to every sense. Take the children outside and do the following activities to help them start building a good vocabulary bank for the future.

Activity 1: Scent pots

Type of activity: Adult-led, whole group.

Resources: Plastic cups, access to a range of natural resources, fresh air (our scents were overpowered by muck spreading in nearby fields!).

What to do: Give the children a plastic cup each. Take them outside and explain that you would like them to search for natural objects that have a smell. The children should collect these items in their cups to create scent pots.

As the children go about picking things to put in their cups, talk to them and help them to describe what the contents smell like. Encourage them to compare the difference between dry, wet and damp items. Show them how to crush flower heads and grass to release juices and stronger scents. Allow them to use sticks to mix the contents of their pots and see what happens.

Key vocabulary: Flower, petal, blossom, grass, soil, earth, mud, damp, wet, dry, crush, squeeze, juice, smell, scent, strong, faint, musky, musty, fresh, sweet, earthy, grassy, damp, different, stinky, horrible, nice, fragrant, perfume.

Extension ideas: Take the scent pots back to the setting and ask the children to give you some words to describe the smells. Write the words on small stickers and stick them to the sides of the pots.

Collect some natural outdoor scents.

Activity 2: Sharing a Shell

Type of activity: Adult-initiated, during independent play.

Resources: Rocks, pebbles, shells, plastic fish tank plants, toy fish, starfish and seagull or bird, plastic tub and cup, toy crab, sea anemone (find these in pet shops for fish tanks) and bristle worm (find rubber worms with bristles in toy shops), large shells.

What to do: Turn the water tray into a rock pool. Sprinkle sand across the bottom and set out the above toys and resources. Bring some children together to read *Sharing a Shell* by Julia Donaldson and Lydia Monks. Show them the water tray and introduce the characters. Act out the story together using the props and emphasise Donaldson's use of prepositions and verbs in the retelling.

Key vocabulary: Inside, outside, under, in, on, too small, bigger, heavy, climb, move, running, rocketing, roaming, scuttling, romping, wiggling.

Extension ideas: Can the children think of any other words to describe how crabs, fish and birds move?

Activity 3: Listen and move

Type of activity: Adult-led, small groups (to avoid collisions).

Resources: Large open space.

What to do: Take the children out to a large space and explain that they should listen to and follow your instructions to practise moving around in different ways.

Begin by instructing the children to walk around slowly. Follow this up with instructions to stop, start, move faster, slower and change direction. Once the children have got the gist of the game, invite volunteers to come out to the front and call out the instructions.

Key vocabulary: Move, fast, slow, speed up, slow down, turn, stop, start, change direction.

Extension ideas: Introduce different movements such as spinning, twirling, jumping, hopping and skipping. Give the children ribbons, hoops and balls and encourage them to describe their movements.

Try...

...making a texture trail. Send the children to find soft, hard, rough, smooth, brittle, bumpy and slimy natural objects and materials. Lay the objects on the floor and invite the children to walk over them in bare feet and describe how they feel.

Visit a park and add words that describe play, nature and the elements to your vocabulary bank.

Activity 4: Feely buckets

Type of activity: Adult-initiated, during independent play.

Resources: Five buckets, string, black bin liners, scissors, access to a range of natural items and materials.

What to do: Fill five buckets with different natural objects and materials, for example, moss, gravel, mud, sticks, grass, leaves and sand. Add different substances and materials to the items in the buckets to change how they feel. For instance, add water to make the mud sloppy or to make the moss wet and spongy; add sand to the grass to make it feel rough and grainy; add gravel to the sand to make it lumpy; and add soil to the leaves to make them damp and sticky. Cover each bucket with a black bin liner and tie it around the rim with string, then cut a slit in the top.

Bring children over to the buckets and invite them to stick their hands in and feel what is inside. Ask them to describe what it feels like. Can they say what is inside each bucket?

Key vocabulary: Feel, touch, rough, smooth, wet, slimy, sticky, sandy, grainy, gritty, sloppy, spongy, soft, damp, dry, crunchy, crumbly.

Extension ideas: Fill the buckets with unusual substances such as slime, flax seed, porridge oats mixed with water, cooked spaghetti and oil and wet sponges.

Activity 5: Park life

Type of activity: Whole group visit.

Resources: Transport and adult supervision for a trip off-site.

What to do: Take a trip to the park and take advantage of all the different aspects of park life to experience a wide range of activities and learn a range of words to name and describe the things that you see and do. Play in a playground, follow a nature trail, fly kites, have a picnic, spot wildlife and talk about the weather.

Key vocabulary: Play, jump, run, climb, swing, balance, fast, slow, leaves, conkers, acorns, grass, soft, damp, rough, smooth, wet, dry, cold, warm, rainy, sunny, drizzle, puddle, splash, mud, dirty, windy, fly, high, drift, float, breeze, bird, duck, squirrel, dog, picnic, taste, favourite, flavour.

Extension ideas: Read poems about nature and park life on your return to the setting.

Don't forget to think about...

...using a wide vocabulary around young children. The more words they hear, the more they will learn. The meaning is often conveyed in the context of the sentence and if they do not understand they will ask you what you mean.

Activity 6: Fire!

Type of activity: Whole group visit.

Resources: Transport and adult supervision for a trip off-site.

What to do: Take the children to visit a fire station where they can see a real fire engine, dress in a real uniform and experience holding a real fire hose. The children will absorb a wide range of vocabulary to do with vehicles, fire-fighting equipment, emergency protocols and water.

Key vocabulary: Fire, emergency, siren, alarm, engine, drive, wheels, ladder, climb, equipment, uniform, helmet, boots, heatproof, protection, high visibility, mask, oxygen, tank, hose, water, gush, power, pressure, spray.

Extension ideas: Create a display about the visit on your return to the setting. Print off photos and ask the children to help write descriptive captions for each.

Enhancing continuous provision

Sue Palmer and Ros Bayley (2013) offer some good advice about helping children to extend their language and learn new vocabulary during independent play. They advise against rushing into and interrupting play situations with loads of questions, but instead suggest standing back and observing before subtly joining in. Among other suggestions, Palmer and Bayley advocate the use of 'pole-bridging talk', whereby practitioners quietly talk to themselves and describe what they are doing just like the children do when they are playing. This self-talk will gradually pique the children's interest, drawing them to the adult and opening up the opportunity for conversation and language extension.

The ideas in the table below aim to demonstrate how everyday enhancements provide opportunities for building and developing an ever-widening vocabulary.

Area of provision	Enhancements that help children to build a vocabulary
Water	Add different substances to the water tray to give it a variety of appearances and textures. Make slime with soapflakes, add washing up liquid to create bubbles, make some jelly, freeze blocks of ice, add food colouring and essence. Provide whisks, sieves, jugs, beakers and waterwheels for the children to play and explore. Key vocabulary: feel, thick, run, trickle, gloopy, slimy, sloppy, pour, froth, bubble, mix, whisk, smell, scent, hard, cold, smooth, chip, empty, full.
Sand	Add special objects/materials/substances to the sand. Mix in glitter, rice or coloured pasta. Bury jewels, precious stones or coins. Add slime, soapy water or cornflour and water mix. Key vocabulary: texture, feeling, gritty, damp, wet, slimy, frothy, sparkly, glittery, shiny, coarse, rough, dry.
Construction	Provide large hollow blocks, wooden bricks, crates and planks. Key vocabulary: build, position, next to, on top, straight, curved, tall, low, high, stack, balance.
Role Play	Mud café: Set up a table with containers, sticks, tubs, pots, soil, mud and real cooking utensils such as pots, pans, spatulas and wooden spoons. Key vocabulary: mud, mix, add, wet, sloppy, pie, mould, form, dry, soft, hard, dirty.
Investigation	Provide bug catchers, magnifiers, digital cameras and minibeast identification charts for the children to capture and observe small creatures. Key vocabulary: minibeast, insect, creature, crawl, scuttle, fly, creep, small, large, colour, pattern, legs, head, antennae, wings, slither, shell, slime, flutter.
Physical	Print, laminate and display the words to the song Here we go round the mulberry bush. Gather some children, form a circle and introduce the song. Encourage the children to think of different actions they perform in the morning. Leave the children to sing together. Key vocabulary: wake, bed, brush, hair, teeth, eat, breakfast, walk, scoot, play, school, nursery, pre-school.
Garden	Set out some sorting baskets and collections of pebbles, flowers, conkers, seeds, twigs and leaves for the children to sort and classify according to their own criteria. Key vocabulary: colour, shape, round, long, short, thin, wide, big, small.

Curriculum links

Building a vocabulary covers the following areas of learning and development:

EYFS	Develops an understanding of simple concepts; learns new words very rapidly and is able to use them in communicating; builds up a vocabulary that reflects the breadth of their experiences; extends vocabulary, especially by grouping and naming, exploring the meaning and sounds of new words (CL). Uses vocabulary and forms of speech that are increasingly influenced by experiences of books (L).
NIC	Names and describes; takes part/contributes to group oral language activities; expresses themselves with increasing clarity and confidence, using a growing vocabulary and more complex sentence structure (LL).
SCE	Extends and enriches vocabulary through listening, talking, watching and reading; listens and takes part in conversations and discussions, and discovers new words and phrases to help express ideas, thoughts and feelings; explores words, discovering how they work together (LE).
WFPF	Uses appropriate language in spontaneous and structured play activities and when conveying meaning; chooses words deliberately; extends vocabulary through activities that encourage interest in words (LLC).

Understanding

Vocabulary and language are central to a developing knowledge and understanding of the world. Children use language to internalise, process, retain and recall information. In the early years we can help children develop a good understanding of basic concepts by introducing descriptive language within meaningful contexts.

Understanding involves the following skills and concepts:

- Understanding that language conveys meaning

- Being able to focus, concentrate and maintain attention

- Understanding and recognising basic nouns, verbs, prepositions and concepts

- Being able to respond appropriately to words and signs

- Being able to answer questions

- Being able to follow increasingly complex instructions.

Help children practise absorbing and processing language by planning activities and games that require them to think about and respond to what they hear.

The following are suggestions for some straightforward activities that ask the children to quietly observe, listen and respond, as well as some fun, active games that take advantage of the outdoor space to get them processing information to accurately follow instructions.

Activity 1: Simon says

Type of activity: Adult-led, whole group.

Resources: Large space.

What to do: Take the children outside to a large open space, ask them to spread out and play a game of Simon says.

Explain that you are going to call out different instructions. If you say 'Simon says' the children must carry out the instruction. However, if you call out an instruction without saying 'Simon says' they must ignore the instruction and stand still.

If a child carries out an instruction when they are not meant to they should sit out of the game. The winner is the child remaining at the end.

Key vocabulary: Simon says, listen, instruction, copy.

Extension ideas: Choose volunteers to come to the front and be Simon.

Play games that require children to listen to, understand and follow instructions.

Activity 3: Toss the beanbag

Type of activity: Adult-led, groups of up to 10.

Resources: Red, green, yellow and blue coloured large hula-hoops (at least three of each colour), red, green, yellow and blue coloured bean-bags (at least 10 of each colour).

What to do: Lay out the hula-hoops and beanbags on the floor of a large open space. Bring the children together and explain that when you call out a colour you would like them to run and grab the corresponding coloured beanbags and put them in the same coloured hoops. Play this game a few times.

Move the beanbags out of the hoops and play a more difficult version of the game. This time explain you are going to call out one colour, followed by a different colour. The children should pick up beanbags that are the first colour and put them in hoops that are the second colour.

Key vocabulary: Listen carefully, instruction.

Extension ideas: Make the game more difficult again by using sounds to represent colours. For example, ring a bell for red, clap hands for yellow, blow a whistle for green and bang a drum for blue.

Activity 2: Tell a story

Type of activity: Adult-led, whole group.

Resources: Comfortable outside space with a soft (grassy) surface for sitting on.

What to do: Take the children to a nice comfortable outside space and tell them a story without the use of a book or props. Stand up in front of them and tell the story from memory. Use different voices, move around and use gestures, facial expressions and body language to enhance the telling. Traditional tales are often best because they are easy to remember with repeated refrains and larger-than-life characters.

When you have finished telling the story, sit down and engage the children in a discussion about what happened. Talk about the different characters, what they did and the consequences of their actions. Ask the children what might have happened if a key event had happened in a different way. Ask them if they enjoyed the ending or if they would have liked something different to happen.

Key vocabulary: Listen, tell, what happened? what if? character, favourite, like, dislike, how? why? why not?

Extension ideas: Alter stories and change endings to see how the children respond.

Challenge the children to listen to verbal descriptions and find matching objects.

Activity 4: Body language

Type of activity: Adult-led, small groups.

Resources: Picture cards featuring faces showing different emotions (find many examples on the internet).

What to do: Take the children out to a quiet space. Explain that when we communicate with each other we use more than just words; we also send messages through our faces and bodies. Give the children an example such as shouting in an angry voice, with an angry facial expression, whilst stamping your foot. Give each child a picture card featuring a facial expression that conveys an emotion such as happy, sad, angry, tired, excited and scared. Ask each child in turn to show the emotion on their card using their voice, face and body.

Key vocabulary: Feelings, emotions, face, expression, words, voice, sound, body, movement, stance, gesture.

Extension ideas: Turn the activity into a game of charades whereby each child takes a turn to convey an emotion using their face and body but no words, whilst the other children guess how they are feeling.

Activity 5: Go seek and find

Type of activity: Adult-initiated, during independent play.

Resources: Woodland or garden area with access to a range of natural objects, timer, whistle.

What to do: Gather a small group of children and explain that you are going to play a seek and find game. Explain that you are going to ask them to find a range of different objects one at a time. They will need to listen very carefully to your description and take care to find exactly what you have described. They have until the timer runs out to find each object, and you will blow the whistle to tell them when the time is up.

What you send the children to find will depend upon where you play the game. Try to include two or three features for each object. Some ideas include; a large open pinecone, three small stones, a yellow and white flower and a twig with a leaf attached. If you do not have access to such objects, send them to find different outdoor toys and resources, for example; a large blue boat, a small yellow spade, a four wheeled vehicle and a green spotted ball.

Key vocabulary: Listen carefully, look, find, as described.

Extension ideas: Invite the children to send each other off to seek and find items of their choosing.

Try...

...displaying open-ended questions on the inside of windows facing out into the outdoor area. Use these as prompts when facilitating discussion between children.

Activity 6: Capture the flag

Type of activity: Adult-led, groups of up to six.

Resources: Large open space, two different coloured hula hoops, ten beanbags (in two different colours to match the hoops – five of each colour), five minute timer.

What to do: Take the children out to a large space and play 'Capture the flag'. Place a different coloured hula hoop at each end of the space. Put five matching coloured beanbags inside each hoop. Divide the children into two small teams and stand each team next to a hoop. Explain they must run to the other team's hoop, take one beanbag and race back to put it in their own hoop. Once all the beanbags have been captured and swapped the children must try to capture them back and return them to the original hoops. Give the children five minutes to play. The winning team is the one with the most matching coloured beanbags in their hoop when the time runs out.

Key vocabulary: Listen, instruction, rules, aim of the game.

Extension ideas: Play more games that involve understanding instructions and following rules, such as 'Stuck in the mud' or 'Cat and mouse'.

Enhancing continuous provision

Practitioners can also support children's developing understanding by helping to interpret and give meaning to the world around them during everyday experiences and activities. This means engaging the children in conversation and introducing basic nouns, verbs, prepositions and concepts. In the table below are just a few suggestions for a range of resources and materials that can be used to do this (these are by no means exhaustive). Chat with the children as they play. Talk about and describe the resources they are using and make observations about what they are doing. Encourage them to talk about what is happening and why. Join the play and allow the children to give you and each other explanations and instructions.

Area of provision	Enhancements that help children to build a general understanding
Water	Provide a range of different sized bottles and shaped containers for the children to pour water from and into. Provide the resources needed to build a waterway including pipes, tubes, funnels, guttering, jugs, crates and hurdle stands. Opportunities to explore: size, shape, position, capacity, volume, materials.
Sand	Provide a range of different shaped buckets and sand moulds for the children to fill and build castles, pictures and sculptures. Supply dry, damp and wet sand. Bury jewels, coins, dinosaur bones and random objects, and provide sieves and spades to dig them up. Opportunities to explore: size, shape, position, capacity, volume, texture, materials, colour.
Construction	Provide a variety of different construction materials. Supply role-play builder's hard hats, high-visibility jackets and tools to get the children talking, discussing with and responding to each other. Opportunities to explore: size, shape, position, design, colour, prepositions.
Role Play	Three bears cottage: In the playhouse lay a table with three different sized bowls, set out three different sized chairs and make up three different sized beds. Provide three cuddly toy father, mother and baby bears. Opportunities to explore: size, emotions, relationships, motives.
Investigation	Start a collection of unusual objects. Ask the children to bring things in from home and set up an outdoor 'found items' display. These could include engine parts, natural items or building materials. Take a close look at the features of the different objects and talk about the purpose of each. Opportunities to explore: shape, size, colour, form, materials, purpose.
Physical	Set up an obstacle course. Give the children balls, quoits, hoops, beanbags, stilts and skipping ropes. Opportunities to explore: movement, position, balance, apparatus, size, shape, direction.
Garden	Plant flowers and vegetables. Place windmills, gnomes, garden ornaments and solar lamps around and about. Opportunities to explore: colour, shape, light, weather, growth, life, decay.

Curriculum links

Understanding covers the following areas of learning and development:

EYFS	Follows instructions involving several ideas or actions; listens to and responds to ideas expressed by others in conversation or discussion; develops an understanding of simple concepts; understands 'who', 'what', 'where' in simple questions; answers 'how' and 'why' questions about their experiences and in response to stories or events (CL).
NIC	Understands non-verbal signals; takes part and contributes to group oral language activities; answers questions to give information and demonstrate understanding; listens to and carries out increasingly complex instructions; listens with increasing attentiveness and for longer periods of time (LL).
SCE	Listens and watches for useful or interesting information and uses this to make choices or learn new things; to help understand stories and other texts, asks questions and links learning with what they already know (LE).
WFPF	Listens to and carries out instructions; listens and responds appropriately and effectively, with growing attention and concentration; in explanations, descriptions and narratives, incorporates relevant detail and identifies what is essential; asks and answers questions (LLC).

Developing spoken language

Young children learn to talk by listening to and copying others and using this to develop their own spoken language. In the early years it is important to give children plenty of opportunities to hear spoken language modelled in a variety of contexts.

What's more, it is also crucial to give children time and space to reflect upon what they hear and formulate their own responses. In other words, practitioners need to have the confidence to embrace the silence and give children a chance to think and find the words they need to respond.

Developing spoken language involves the following skills and concepts:

● Understanding that language conveys meaning

● Being able to form clear speech sounds

● Being able to listen to and copy others

● Being able to listen to and respond appropriately to others

● Understanding and being able to use a range of words and phrases to convey meaning.

As previously mentioned, children absorb language better if it is contextualised through meaningful concrete experiences.

The following are a variety of methods that practitioners can use outdoors to help children gain confidence and develop their speech and language skills.

Method 1: Fairies at the bottom of the garden

Purpose: To use small-world play to capture the children's imaginations, making it easier to absorb and use language.

Resources: Toy fairies, toadstools, miniature huts, houses and castles, glitter, flower patch.

What to do: Set up a fairy garden in and around some flowers and leafy plants. Place miniature buildings and toadstools around and about. Sit and stand fairies amongst the flowers. Sprinkle glitter all over. When the children discover it pretend to be none the wiser. Allow them to speculate as to where the fairies have come from. Join the children's play and help to create a storyline filled with magical vocabulary.

More ideas: Suggest the fairies may come alive at night and create proof that this might be happening by leaving clues and evidence around the outdoor area for the children to discover on their arrival each morning.

Use puppets to engage children in conversation outside.

Method 2: Ebenezer Growmore the gardener

Purpose: To use an outdoor character puppet that will engage and entertain the children, making them want to listen and talk.

Resources: A large puppet.

What to do: Use a large puppet when working in the outdoor growing area, call it Ebenezer Growmore! Explain that Ebenezer is a very knowledgeable gardener and use it to introduce gardening activities. Then, as the children are working and playing, carry the puppet around to talk with them and offer snippets of information and advice about what they are doing. Encourage the children to ask the puppet any questions they may have about growing.

More ideas: Give the puppet something new and interesting to show the children each week. It could be an unusual vegetable, a gardening tool, plant or book.

Method 3: Place to talk

Purpose: To create a quiet space outdoors where children are able to listen to and develop spoken language.

Resources: Permanent structure, such as a wooden shed or temporary shelter, such as a gazebo with roll down sides.

What to do: Set up a comfortable and inviting shelter or quiet outside space to make focused group talk time possible outdoors. Take small groups to the shelter on a regular basis to look at interesting objects or talk about recent happenings and events. Ensure the groups are small enough so that everyone has a chance to join in and are able to concentrate and listen to others speak.

More ideas: Set up tents, dens and shelters for the children to take themselves away from the hustle and bustle of outdoor play and have a quiet chat between themselves.

Try...

...displaying prompt cards in each area of provision with key questions and vocabulary for practitioners to refer to when fostering conversation (see the sustained shared thinking cards in The Project Approach *by Marianne Sargent, published by Practical Pre-School Books).*

Create a comfortable outdoor shelter for focused group talk time.

Use everyday activities to give language meaning.

Method 5: From table to plate

Purpose: To use everyday tasks and activities to contextualise language and give it meaning, making it easier to learn.

Resources: Growing area or planters, compost, gardening tools and equipment, seeds.

What to do: Help the children to grow their own food. Plant and cultivate seeds to produce vegetables and herbs.

Get the children fully involved, all the time explaining what different tools are and what they are for.

Talk about the vegetables you are growing, what they will look like, what they can be used for and how they can be eaten. Start up conversations about favourite foods and flavours.

Smell the herbs you grow, and talk about the scents.

Ask the children what types of fruit and vegetables they eat and how they are prepared at home.

More ideas: Harvest and cook the fruits and vegetables you grow. Cook them outside on a barbecue or camp fire as well as indoors using a stove. Compare how they taste using the different methods.

Method 4: Repeat after me

Purpose: To help children learn language structures that they can build upon and develop themselves.

Resources: Enough space to play parachute games, parachute, large lightweight ball.

What to do: Play active parachute games that involve the use of repetitive phrases. Try for example:

Parachute cross over – the whole group holds on to the parachute and raises it into the air as the practitioner instructs all those who have brown hair, red shoes, skirts, etc to run under the parachute and across to the other side. Repeat the phrase, 'Run girls, run boys, everyone else make some noise!' each time the children cross over.

Making waves – the whole group lifts their arms up and down to create ripples and waves in the fabric, then lifts the parachute into the air to tuck themselves underneath at the finish. Chant the following phrase, 'Up and down, ripple and roll, up in the air and under we go.'

Bouncy ball – everyone works together to keep a large lightweight ball bouncing by flapping the parachute up and down. Chant the following phrase, 'Bounce, bounce, bounce the ball, don't give up, don't let it fall.'

I like sausages – everyone waves the parachute up and down while singing, 'I like sausages, I like beans, but I don't like sherbet 'cause it makes me sneeze.' Everyone then shouts, 'Atishoo!' and lifts the parachute up in the air. Each time a child takes their turn to run under the parachute shouting, 'My favourite food is…because…'

My best friends – the whole group holds on to the parachute and sings the following, 'My best friends are always there, we play and laugh and show we care.' Then everyone lifts the parachute in the air while a nominated child runs underneath and says, 'I like Charlie because…'

More ideas: Introduce rhymes and phrases that can be repeated and elaborated upon for other outdoor activities such as jumping in puddles, chasing leaves and playing chasing or ball games.

HOME LINKS

Take photos of your outdoor activities throughout the course of each week and paste them onto a 'This week we have been…' sheet. Print one off at the end of each week and send a copy home with each child. Ask parents to use the sheet to talk with their children about what they have been doing and learning.

Enhancing continuous provision

Create a learning environment that is full of conversation and discussion by exposing children to a wide range of experiences that will capture their interest. Try setting up provocations that stir the children's imagination, excite them and encourage them to talk. In the table below are some suggestions for provocations, as well as openers and comments that practitioners can use to start conversations and trigger discussion.

Area of provision	Provocation ideas and helpful conversation openers that aim to encourage children to talk
Water	Frozen: Freeze some large blocks of ice with random objects inside and leave them in the water tray for the children to examine and investigate. Useful comments: I wonder how long it will take for that big piece of ice to melt. If I keep my fingers on the ice it feels like they are sticking to it. Look at all the water in the bottom of the tray.
Sand	The thing: Use a large cardboard template cut into the shape of big feet and use it to create a trail of footprints across the sand pit. Useful comments: Wow, those are large footprints! I wonder where they came from. I have never seen a creature with feet that big before.
Construction	Who lives in a house like this?: Create a small den out of natural materials. Make a bed using moss and leaves and a table and chairs using pieces of wood and bark. Leave if for the children to discover. Useful comments: Well that is an unusual little house. I wonder what it is like to sleep somewhere like that.
Role Play	Abandoned loot: Leave a swag bag full of costume jewellery and toy money hidden somewhere in the outdoor area. Let the children discover it and act surprised. Provide role-play robber and police costumes and equipment for the children to develop the theme. Useful comments: Well that's very strange. I wonder where that came from.
Investigation	Inner workings: Enable the children to inspect the cross-sections of some natural objects and materials with magnifiers. For example, a clean piece of honeycomb, a sliced log, a conker inside its outer shell cut in half and an open pea pod. Useful comments: Look at that pattern. I wonder what that is. Let's get a closer look.
Physical	Box of balls: Fill a large container with a variety of balls, for example, footballs, tennis balls, pingpong balls, beach balls, golf balls, rubber balls and airflow balls. Join in as the children play with them. Useful comments: I wonder why I can't get this ball to bounce very high. Wow, look how far you managed to throw that ball! It looks like that ball could float away.
Garden	Where the wind blows: Place windmills, wind socks, ribbons, streamers and wind chimes all around the garden; stuck in the soil, tied to tree branches, hanging off fences and loose in large tubs for the children to pick out and play with. Useful comments: Look how it moves in the breeze. What a lovely sound. Crikey it's windy today.

Curriculum links

Developing spoken language covers the following areas of learning and development:

EYFS	Begins to use more complex sentences to link thoughts; uses a range of tenses; uses vocabulary focused on objects and people that are of particular importance to them; uses language to imagine and recreate roles and experiences in play situations; links statements and sticks to a main theme or intention; introduces a storyline or narrative to their play (CL).
NIC	Repeats familiar phrases; talks about experiences, pictures and stories; talks about work, play and things they have made; describes; takes part/contributes to group oral language activities; expresses themselves with increasing clarity and confidence, using a growing vocabulary and more complex sentence structure (LL).
SCE	When listening and taking part in conversations and discussions, discovers new words and phrases to help express ideas, thoughts and feelings (LE).
WFPF	Uses appropriate language in spontaneous and structured play activities and when conveying meaning; talks/communicates, spontaneously and through structured activities, for a variety of purposes, including: repeating rhymes and poems, sometimes from memory, telling and retelling stories, both real and imagined, talking of matters of immediate and personal interest; participates in role play and imaginative play (LLC).

Expressing thoughts and ideas

Being able to understand and use expressive language is fundamental to the development of creative and critical thinking skills. Children who have what the EYFS terms as 'the language of thinking and learning' are more able to process information, make connections, form opinions and think of ideas. What's more, they are better at verbalising their thoughts and discussing their ideas with others, which is important for evaluating, coming up with solutions and making reasoned decisions.

Expressing thoughts and ideas involves the following skills and concepts:

● Being able to retain and recall useful information

● Understanding and being able to use a range of words and phrases to convey meaning

● Being able to organise, sequence and clarify thoughts

● Being able to explain what is happening and predict what will happen next

● Being able to listen to and respond appropriately to others.

In order to help children learn a range of expressive language, practitioners should plan hands-on active experiences that foster conversation and get children questioning. Practitioners can also use carefully considered questions to guide the children through different thought processes, as well as to generate debate and discussion and get them using a range of different thinking skills.

Activity 1: What's the problem?

Type of activity: Adult-initiated, during independent play.

Resources: Digital camera.

What to do: Help the children to reflect, recount and evaluate by observing and highlighting problems they come across in their outdoor play.

Take photos and film of the children who are encountering problems, such as not having enough space to play a game, not having the correct equipment to carry out a particular task or struggling to build or construct something.

Later take the children involved to one side and show them the photos or film you took. Ask them to explain what the problem was, and if they found a solution. Ask them to think about what they might have done differently if they encountered the problem again.

Key questions: What were you doing? What happened when…? What could you have done? Why do you think that happened? Is there anything else you could have used? Why didn't that work?

Extension ideas: Use a projector to show the photos or film to the whole group and invite other children to offer ideas and suggestions.

Encourage children to think about and suggest solutions to the problems they encounter during their play.

Activity 2: The odd egg

Type of activity: Adult-initiated, during independent play.

Resources: Twigs, straw, thin needle, black/brown thread, large balloon, newspaper, PVA glue, thick paint brushes, paint, string, ladder.

What to do: Make a very large nest by weaving and tying some twigs and straw together with thread. Make a very large egg by sticking pieces of torn up newspaper onto a blown up balloon with PVA glue. Paint the egg an unusual colour and coat it in watered down PVA glue to make it more durable in damp weather. Use a needle and thread to attach the egg to the nest. Place the nest high in a tree or on a roof and tie it securely in place with some string.

Key questions: What do you think might be inside that egg? What do you think might lay an egg like that? Have you ever seen anything like that before?

Extension ideas: Show the children a range of real eggs such as chicken, quail, duck, goose and ostrich. Compare the colours, sizes, patterns and weights and ask the children to think about what birds they could have come from.

Activity 3: The cocoon

Type of activity: Adult-initiated, during independent play.

Resources: Very large cereal box, coloured tissue paper, scissors, PVA glue, thick paint brushes, string, ladder.

What to do: Make a large colourful cocoon using a cereal box covered in multicoloured tissue paper. Coat the entire cocoon in watered down PVA glue to make it more durable in damp weather. Thread through a piece of string and hang it high up out of reach, for instance in a tree or from a gutter in the outdoor area.

Leave it for the children to discover and let them speculate as to what it is and where it has come from.

Key questions: What do you think it might be? Where do you think it came from? Do you think there is anything inside? Have you seen anything like that before?

Extension ideas: Place a creature nestled in shredded tissue paper inside the cocoon and gradually split it open over a course of a week.

Try…

…helping children to self-evaluate and reassess their thinking by assisting them in putting their ideas into action even if you know they will not work.

Involve the children in designing and building a minibeast hotel.

Activity 5: Minibeast hotel

Type of activity: Adult-led, small groups.

Resources: Wooden pallets, tree bark, bamboo, leaves, soil, grass, information books about minibeasts.

What to do: Bring the children together and explain that you would like to encourage more minibeasts to move into the area. Look at information books and talk about the different habitats that minibeasts like to live in. Tell the children that you already have some wooden pallets and pieces of bamboo and ask them to suggest what else they could use to build a minibeast hotel. Collect some natural materials and help the children to construct the hotel, giving them as much free reign as possible.

Key questions: What do you think we need? Where does that insect like to live? Why do you think they like to live there? Does that look safe and secure? What might happen if you put that there? Why isn't that working?

Extension ideas: See what moves in and discuss why the hotel has attracted those particular minibeasts. Help the children to consider how they might alter or add to the hotel to make it more attractive to others.

HOME LINKS

Give families a homework challenge that involves working together to build a den at home or in a nearby park. This is an open-ended challenge so parents can use whatever is at their disposal, including outdoor garden furniture, tents and large sticks. Ask parents to take photos of the process and send them in to the setting with their children to show and tell.

Activity 4: Teddy bears' picnic

Type of activity: Adult-led, whole group.

Resources: Adult supervision for trips to the local shop/supermarket and park, teddy bears, picnic blankets, picnic bags/boxes, food preparation equipment, picnic plates and cups.

What to do: Involve the children in planning a teddy bears' picnic. Help them decide where to go, how to get there and what to eat, then write a shopping list, go out to buy the food, prepare and pack it.

Throughout the process help the children consider how they are going to go about each task, including planning what they need to do and how they can get everything they need. Discuss picnic locations and evaluate them according to how easy it is to get there, whether they are suitable locations for picnics and if there is any play equipment. Decide what to take including suitable clothing and toys. Get the children to help compose a letter to parents about the trip and asking them to send in the children's teddy bears.

Key questions: What do we need to do first? What do we need to do next? Why do we need to do that? Is there anything we have forgotten? How do you think we should do this?

Extension ideas: Share photos of the picnic with the children and reflect upon how it went. Is there anything the children would like to do differently next time?

Involve the children in planning, preparing and going on a teddy bears' picnic.

Enhancing continuous provision

Provide a range of resources and materials and use playground chalks or easels to set out challenges that will get the children thinking about how they can approach different tasks. As the children play, ask them to explain what they are doing. Assist them and take instructions from them. Sensitively question their ideas and encourage them to discuss their thoughts with each other.

Area of provision	Enhancements that encourage children to express thoughts and ideas
Water	Build a waterway with hurdle stands, crates, pipes and guttering. Ensure that part of the waterway travels uphill. Give the children ping-pong balls, jugs and buckets of water and challenge them to get the balls from one end of the waterway to the other. Key questions: Why won't the ball go that way? What do you think you can do about that? Why did the ball fall off?
Sand	Mix some sand with coloured glitter and PVA glue and fill it into sand moulds. Leave them to set then turn out the solid sparkly sand sculptures and bury them in the sand tray or pit and leave them for the children to discover. Key questions: What is that? How do you think they were made? Where do you think they came from? Do you think you could make one of those?
Construction	Set out some stacks of large crates and challenge the children to build a den. Make stipulations such as, it must be tall enough to stand inside, have a roof, a door and two windows. Key questions: Is that safe? Why didn't that work? What are you trying to do? Can you think of another way?
Role Play	Set up a stage with chairs for an audience. Supply a variety of costumes, props and musical instruments for the children to plan and stage their own performances. Key questions: What role are you playing? What are you going to use that for? What do you think you could use for…?
Investigation	Draw out a huge pirate treasure map on the floor using playground chalk. Strategically place small islands, palm trees, rocks, huts, sharks and ships. Draw on a cross to show where the treasure is buried. Provide some toy boats and set challenges to find the quickest route from certain points to the treasure, while avoiding particular places or obstacles. Key questions: Why are you sure that is the quickest way? Have you tried any other routes? What if you tried…?
Physical	Draw out a maze on the floor of a wide open space using playground chalks with routes to a number of different objects that are placed inside. Challenge the children to work out how to get to each object. Key questions: Is that the easiest way to get there? What if you turned the other way? Which is the easiest to get to? Can you explain how you got there? Can you draw your own maze?
Garden	Fasten sticks and twigs together into cross shapes. Provide strips of hessian, long grass, small pine cones, straw, string and scissors. Challenge the children to make bird scarers for the growing area. Key questions: What do you think will scare the birds? How are you going to attach that to the stick? Can you think of anything else you could use?

Curriculum links

Expressing thoughts and ideas covers the following areas of learning and development:

EYFS	Uses talk to connect ideas, explain what is happening and anticipate what might happen next, recall and relive past experiences; questions why things happen and gives explanations; links statements and sticks to a main theme or intention; uses talk to organise, sequence and clarify thinking, ideas, feelings and events; develops own narratives and explanations by connecting ideas or events (CL).
NIC	Talks about work, play and things they have made; expresses themselves with increasing clarity and confidence, using a growing vocabulary and more complex sentence structure; answers questions to give information and demonstrate understanding; asks questions to find information or seek an explanation; offers reasons to support opinions given (LL).
SCE	Listens or watches for useful or interesting information and uses it to make choices or learn new things; within real and imaginary situations, shares experiences and feelings, ideas and information in a way that communicates their message (LE).
WFPF	Builds on previous experience, speaks confidently, and makes themselves clear by: organising what they say, choosing words deliberately, relating their contributions in discussion to what has gone on before by taking similar/different views into account, and using the conventions of discussion and conversation; in their explanations, descriptions and narratives, incorporates relevant detail and identifies what is essential; expresses thoughts, ideas and feelings, likes, dislikes and needs; expresses opinions (LLC).

Interacting with others

Having the ability to listen attentively, process the information heard and respond appropriately is essential for social interaction. However, there are also a number of social skills that young children need to learn early on if they are to successfully interact with others. From the listener's point of view this includes maintaining eye contact, sitting or standing still and attending to the speaker without interrupting. From the speaker's point of view this means engaging the listener by speaking in a clear and understandable way.

Interacting with others involves the following skills and concepts:

● Being able to sit/stand still and maintain eye contact

● Being able to focus, concentrate and maintain attention

● Being able to speak clearly

● Being able to listen to and respond appropriately to what others say

● Understanding when to talk and when to listen (being able to take turns)

● Being able to communicate thoughts and ideas so that the listener understands.

The following activities encourage children to interact with each other. Some are play-based and aim simply to get children talking to each other. Otherwise there are ideas for practising specific social skills, such as making eye contact and listening attentively.

Activity 1: Puppet play

Type of activity: Adult-initiated, during independent play.

Resources: Puppets, outdoor puppet theatre.

What to do: Either set up a purpose-built outdoor puppet theatre or make a temporary one using crates or wooden pallets. Provide person or animal puppets for the children to create their own storylines with. Join the play and model how to use the puppets. Demonstrate turning the puppets to face each other when they are talking and use different voices for each character.

Key vocabulary: Puppet, operate, move, talk, speak, listen, theatre, show.

Extension ideas: Provide materials for the children to make their own puppets. Ask the children to tell you about their puppets.

Use puppets to model conversational skills.

Don't forget to think about…

…modelling good listening and attention when interacting with the children. Stop what you are doing, go down to their level and maintain eye contact with them when they are talking to you.

Activity 3: Friendship stop

Type of activity: Adult-initiated, during independent play.

Resources: Friendship stop sign, small outdoor bench or chairs.

What to do: Put a friendship stop sign in the outdoor area and place a bench or some chairs next to it. Whenever some children have a disagreement that they cannot resolve independently, take them to the friendship stop to talk about what has happened and find a solution together. Encourage the children to each take a turn to give their account and help them to listen to each other without interrupting. If an apology is in order encourage them to make eye contact with each other when saying 'sorry'.

Key vocabulary: Friendship stop, what happened? how do you feel? explain, listen, turn, interrupt, look at, sorry, help, resolve.

Extension ideas: As the children become used to using the friendship stop with an adult encourage them to use it to mediate between themselves without your help.

Activity 2: Magic carpet

Type of activity: Adult-initiated, during independent play.

Resources: Old rug, playground chalks.

What to do: Place an old rug on the floor of the outdoor area and write 'magic carpet' in playground chalk on the floor next to it. Join the children as they play, and chat with them about where the carpet is taking them. Share a story with the children to enhance their play, such as *Winnie's Flying Carpet* by Valerie Thomas and Korky Paul.

Key vocabulary: Where? what? how? magic carpet, travel, fly, destination, go, adventure, tell, story.

Extension ideas: Set up other role-play scenarios that will take the children on an adventure, such as a shipwreck, cave with a secret entrance to another world, tent containing explorer outfits and equipment, abandoned alien spacecraft and moonscape.

Encourage children to talk through their disagreements and find a resolution.

Play I spy with a difference.

Activity 4: Look into my eyes

Type of activity: Adult-led, whole group.

Resources: Large open space.

What to do: Instruct the children to spread out in a large open space. Explain that they must all maintain eye contact with you throughout the game. Each time you look directly at a child they must sit on the floor. If a child is not looking at you when you look at them move onto the next child. The children still standing at the end of the game are out.

Play alternative versions of the game, for example, begin with everyone doing star jumps, then standing still with hands by their sides when you look at them. Or make the game more difficult by looking at one child then another to signal they should join hands and make a pair.

Key vocabulary: Concentrate, focus, watch, look, eyes, eye contact.

Extension ideas: Play the game with small groups and invite children to stand at the front to make eye contact with the others.

Activity 5: I spy

Type of activity: Adult-led, small groups.

Resources: Visually interesting outdoor environment.

What to do: Take the children outside to play I spy with a difference.

Instead of using initial letter sounds as the clue use a descriptive sentence. For example, 'I spy with my little eye a small brown ball on the floor' (conker) or '…something see-through in the wall' (window), or '…a red metal object with wheels' (car). Play the game for a while, giving the children a few examples, then allow them to take turns to spy objects and give descriptions.

Key vocabulary: I spy, eye, look, describe, details, see, colour, shape, material, where? what? listen, guess.

Extension ideas: Play variations of the game such as I hear with my little ears, I smell with my little nose or I feel with my little hands, to get children describing different sounds, scents and textures to each other.

Don't forget to think about...

...the great difficulty some children have with making eye contact. There may be a number of reasons for this, ranging from social and emotional issues or special needs to cultural expectations. If you notice a child having difficulty with making eye contact with you or other children, take time to identify the reasons why before putting them under any further pressure to do so.

Activity 6: Taking turns to talk

Type of activity: Adult-led, small groups.

Resources: Small parachute, large lightweight ball.

What to do: Ask the children to hold the edges of the parachute and move it up and down to roll the ball around. Explain that when you call out a child's name everyone must try to get the ball to that person.

When the person gets the ball they must duck under the parachute, poke their head up through the middle and say a simple sentence, for example, 'My name is Iris and I like digging in the sand.'

Key vocabulary: Parachute, ball, concentrate, focus, speak, turn, look, listen, speaker, listener.

Extension ideas: Play a variation of the game without a ball and where everyone is silent. This time you make eye contact with a child, who goes to the middle of the parachute, says the sentence, then looks at another child who takes their place in the middle to speak and so on.

Enhancing continuous provision

Create a vibrant outdoor area with games and activities that encourage children to play and talk together. Set up interactive games that get the children making up and discussing rules, and provide equipment for team games that involve communicating and cooperating with each other.

Create play scenarios and small world scenes that encourage children to act out roles and narrate stories. Furthermore, set up provocations that prompt discussion.

In addition, provide communication equipment such as mobile phones, microphones, walkie talkies and video cameras that the children can incorporate into their play.

Area of provision	Enhancements that encourage children to interact with each other
Water	Freeze coloured water in jelly moulds to create ice sculptures and place them all around the outdoor area in snowy weather to generate conversation and discussion. Paint targets on the walls and provide water squirters for the children to play target games together.
Sand	Create a small world superhero seaside scene. Press a shallow container into the sand, fill it with water and drop in some toy sharks. Place some large rocks around. Put some play people swimming in the water and on top of the rocks. Provide superhero characters for the children to act out rescuing climbers and swimmers in peril.
Construction	Use large hollow blocks to half-build a big house. Create a collapse scene with a puppet trapped under some blocks. Make an ambulance, police car and fire engine out of painted banana boxes and supply emergency worker uniforms and equipment for the children to take on the different roles of investigating what has happened and rescuing the injured person.
Role Play	Café: Set up some alfresco tables and seating and provide notepads, pens, aprons, play food, cutlery, cooker, trays, plates and cooking utensils. Set up an easel with a pictorial food menu. Taxi cab: Use banana boxes to make a taxi with a large plastic plate for a steering wheel.
Investigation	Fasten funnels to the ends of different length tubes and flexible pipes for the children to use as telephones. Set up a treasure hunt for the children to solve together. Put some fairly tricky clues that lead to each other all around the outdoor area with some hidden treasure at the end.
Physical	Draw hopscotch games on the floor for children to play on, talk about their games and discuss rules together. Provide playground chalks for the children to draw out their own games and explain the rules to each other. Set up two goals and provide a ball for the children to play football.
Garden	Garden centre: Set out plant pots, gardening tools, packets of seeds, dried flowers, garden ornaments and gardening magazines. Put a till on a table with some play money and paper bags with handles. Set up a picnic spot for the children to have shared mealtimes (snack, lunch) outdoors, where they can talk together as they eat.

Curriculum links

Interacting with others covers the following areas of learning and development:

EYFS	Gives their attention to what others say and responds appropriately, while engaged in another activity; holds a conversation, jumping from topic to topic; uses intonation, rhythm and phrasing to make the meaning clear to others; links statements and sticks to a main theme or intention; expresses themselves effectively, showing awareness of listeners' needs (CL).
NIC	Initiates and joins in conversations in pairs or groups; listens and responds to adults and peers; understands and uses social conventions in conversations and pupil initiated interactions; initiates and sustains conversations with adults and peers in the classroom (LL).
SCE	When listening and talking in different situations, is learning to take turns and developing awareness of when to talk and when to listen; within real and imaginary situations, shares experiences and feelings, ideas and information in a way that communicates their message (LE).
WFPF	Listens and responds appropriately and effectively, with growing attention and concentration; speaks clearly, with appropriate intonation in own accent, modifying talk to the requirements of the audience (LLC); recognises the importance of clarity, fluency and interest in effective communication (LLC).

Developing a love of stories

A love of stories helps tremendously with early reading and writing. Children who are regularly read to from a young age will have experienced the joy of hearing a favourite story over and over again until they know it off by heart. They will have learned how to read the pictures and join in with repeated refrains, gradually transitioning from listener to storyteller. They will also have a growing awareness of print and language, having seen a variety of texts and listened to many authorial voices.

These children will be more enthusiastic about learning to read because they will see the value in being able to decode text to reveal a story. What's more, they will have developed greater imagination together with a knowledge of story structure, character and setting, which will spur them on to create stories of their own. These children will also be more enthusiastic writers because they will understand the purpose and have an interest in getting their ideas down on paper.

A love of stories does not just involve sharing picture books. Oral storytelling is just as enjoyable because it brings stories to life. Each telling is as individual as the teller with varying degrees of drama, wit and characterisation. Watching a story being performed is especially valuable for improving concentration and listening skills. Without a book or illustrations, the children are required to actively participate and use their imaginations to picture the scene and conjure up the characters.

The outdoor area can add another dimension to storytelling. This provides an exciting and authentic setting with a range of natural scenery and props that can be used to stimulate the imagination and enhance the experience.

So plan to read, tell and re-enact as many stories as possible outdoors! The following are just a few examples.

Story 1: The Bear's Winter House

Type of activity: Whole group visit.

Resources: Transport and adult supervision for a trip off-site.

What to do: Take a trip to a park or woodland area where there is access to plenty of large sticks that can be used for den building. Take a copy of *The Bear's Winter House* by John Yeoman and Quentin Blake with you and find a comfortable spot to sit and read it to the children. Talk about what Bear used to build his winter house. Can the children spot anything lying around that they can use to build a house like Bear's?

Divide the children into groups, allocate each group an adult and challenge them to build a house like Bear's.

Key vocabulary: Bear, house, winter, den, sticks, big, small, fit, build, gap, fill, moss, leaves, cover, rain, cold, shelter, strong, sturdy, safe.

Extension ideas: Ask the children if they can find anything that would make a comfortable bed for the bear.

Use stories as inspiration for outdoor activities.

Story 2: The Flying Diggers

Type of activity: Adult-led, small groups.

Resources: Toy diggers with backhoe loaders, toy diggers with telescopic handlers, hard hats, keys, toy parrots, crocodiles, tigers and other jungle animals, water tray, plants and foliage.

What to do: Take the children outside to sit on the grass and share *The Flying Diggers* by Ian Whybrow and David Melling. Involve the children in setting up a small world play scene using the plants and foliage outside and toy animals. Provide additional toy jungle animals and vehicles for the children to create their own storylines.

Key vocabulary: Flying, diggers, hard hat, keys, backhoe loader, telescopic handler, emergency, danger, roar, soar, jungle, animals, magic.

Extension ideas: Help the children make a role-play digger using large cardboard boxes and junk. Provide hard hats and keys for them to go on their own digger adventures.

Story 3: Once upon a time...

Type of activity: Whole group or small groups.

Resources: Comfortable area to sit down and enjoy a story.

What to do: Tell the children various well known traditional tales without the use of books. Stand up in front of the children and move around as you tell the stories. Create different voices for each of the characters and change your posture to give each one an individual physical presence. Enhance the telling with open-ended natural props. For example, a stick can be used as a walking stick, umbrella, spade or club; soil can be used as porridge; stones and rocks can be used as bricks, golden nuggets or to make a bridge; and leaves can be used as rain, bedding, food or money.

Key vocabulary: Once upon a time, the end.

Extension ideas: Set up story scenes around the outdoor area to encourage the children to re-enact the different tales. For example, make a bridge that the children can walk over, leave out a picnic basket and hooded red cape, and fill three wheelbarrows with straw, sticks and bricks.

Take the children outside and tell them a story.

Make your own Stick Man.

Story 4: Stick Man

Type of activity: Adult-led, small groups.

Resources: Short thick sticks, string, conkers, sellotape, parcel wrap, scissors, logs, bark, leaves, banana box, Christmas wrapping paper.

What to do: Gather the children on a cold frosty day to read *Stick Man* by Julia Donaldson and Axel Scheffler. Wrap up warm and sit on logs, stools or benches. Help the children use short thick sticks to make some models of Stick Man. Tie the sticks together with string to make arms and legs, and stick conkers on for eyes. Ask the children if they have any ideas about other materials or objects that they could use.

Take the Stick Man models outside and use them to act out scenes from the story, while reciting the repeated refrains. Use the grassy area as a park, the water tray as the river and the sand tray as the beach. Make a model of the Stick family home using logs, bark and leaves, and a model of Santa's sleigh using a banana box and Christmas wrapping paper.

Key vocabulary: Stick Man, stick, twig, mast, sword, book, pen, bow, bat, boomerang.

Extension ideas: Leave the sticks and other craft materials for the children to make Stick Lady and the children. Talk about all the different things that sticks can be used for and discuss the merits of the children's different ideas.

Story 5: Elmer and the Wind

Type of activity: Adult-led, small groups.

Resources: Balloons, newspaper, multicoloured tissue paper cut into large squares, PVA glue, brushes, string, scissors.

What to do: Share the story *Elmer and the Wind* by David McKee. Talk about the exciting adventure that Elmer went on when the wind carried him up into the air. Ask the children how they would feel if the same thing happened to them. What would it be like to look down upon everything from so high up in the air?

Help the children make some papier mâché Elmers to take outside and fly on a windy day. Blow up balloons and cover them in torn up multicoloured tissue paper with watered down PVA glue. Take care to leave the knot of the balloon sticking out. When it is dry, draw on some ears, a trunk, some legs, eyes and a mouth. Tie a long piece of string to the balloon knot.

Key vocabulary: Elmer, wind, fly, gust, breeze, float, blustery.

Extension ideas: Make Elmer windsocks and multicoloured windmills to hang and stick around the outdoor area.

Story 6: Bear Hunt

Type of activity: Adult-initiated, during independent play.

Resources: Clothes horses, wooden dividers, crates, sheets, blankets, mats, bear masks.

What to do: Set up a bear cave for the children to act out the cave scene from *We're Going on a Bear Hunt* by Michael Rosen and Helen Oxenbury. Encourage the children to take turns at being the bear. Join them as they play and recite the words in the story.

Key vocabulary: Bear, hunt, over, under, through, tip toe, grass, mud, river, forest, snowstorm, cave, dark, gloomy.

Extension ideas: Set up some apparatus leading up to the cave for the children to act out moving over, under and through.

Go on a bear hunt.

Enhancing continuous provision

Nowadays it is possible to purchase weatherproof bookcases, portable bookstands, hanging wire bookracks and reading sheds and shelters. Otherwise, make your own by arranging books in crates, putting up pop-up tents and laying out blankets and cushions. As far as possible take time throughout the day to sit and read stories to individuals and groups. There are also some fantastic small world and role-play resources designed for outdoor use. Set up small world scenes amongst the shrubbery, in the sand and water trays and on the grass.

Area of provision	Enhancements that help children to develop a love for stories
Water	Place a large toy shark and a variety of tropical toy fish in the water tray. Add a boat with a fisherman and some netting and leave a copy of *Smiley Shark* by Ruth Galloway. Otherwise set the scene for other fishy stories by the same author such as *Fidgety Fish*, *Tickly Octopus* or *Clumsy Crab*. Fill the water tray with slime and add fantasy creatures and monsters.
Sand	Make the sand tray into a moon scape and add some rocks, a rocket, some toy aliens and small people. Provide a copy of *Man on the Moon* by Simon Bartram. Make the sand tray into a desert island with some toy pirates and treasure chests.
Construction	Set out a wooden train set and a copy of *Little Red Train: Race to the Finish* by Benedict Blathwayt. Provide gravel, stones, sticks, twigs and toy sheep for the children to create obstacles on the tracks. Provide different shaped and sized wooden blocks, vehicles, people and animals for the children to construct their own story scenes.
Role Play	Three Bears Cottage: Turn the playhouse into a cottage with a table and three different sized bowls, chairs and beds. Stone Soup: Provide a large cooking pot with wooden spoons, water, fresh or dried herbs and a variety of stones.
Investigation	Set up a sensory bear hunt trail. Lay out some grass turf and shallow trays containing water, mud and wood chip. Invite the children to remove their shoes and socks and physically experience the sensation of walking over the different surfaces.
Physical	Provide crates, large hollow blocks and planks for the children to build a bridge and act out The Three Billy Goats Gruff. Show the children how to play What's the time Mr Wolf?
Garden	Grow beans and provide small world props and characters for the children to act out Jack and the Beanstalk. Print and laminate character cards from *The Gruffalo* and place them amongst the shrubbery.

Curriculum links

Developing a love for stories covers the following areas of learning and development:

EYFS	Joins in with repeated refrains and anticipates key events and phrases in stories; begins to be aware of the way stories are structured; suggests how the story might end; describes main story settings, events and principle characters; listens to stories with increasing attention and recall; enjoys an increasing range of books (L).
NIC	Reads a range of texts including those composed by themselves and others; sequences stories in reasonable detail using appropriate language; develops auditory and visual discrimination and memory; listens to a range of stories, read to them by adults/other pupils (LL).
SCE	Enjoys exploring and choosing stories and other texts to watch, read or listen to, and can share likes and dislikes; enjoys exploring events and characters in stories and other texts, sharing thoughts in different ways, and invents own, sharing these with others in imaginative ways (LE).
WFPF	Follows stories read to them and responds as appropriate; responds in different ways for different purposes, being able to talk about characters, events, language and information as they predict events and explore meaning ; hears lively readings from a variety of sources; reads and shares books written by significant children's authors, and stories that are challenging in terms of length or vocabulary (LLC).

Becoming aware of print

An important first step towards being able to read and write is becoming aware of print. Initially this means introducing children to the letters of the alphabet and giving them opportunities to hear letter names and play with letter shapes. They should also be made aware of print in the environment, and helped to understand that it carries meaning.

Becoming aware of print involves the following skills and concepts:

● Understanding that print carries meaning

● Being able to distinguish between print and pictures

● Being able to recognise own name

● Understanding that there is a difference and being able to distinguish between letters and numerals

● Understanding that in English, print is composed of 26 letters of the alphabet

● Being able to recite the alphabet.

Some children spend the majority of their day outside so it is essential to display print and the letters of the alphabet around the outdoor area. Mount a weatherproof display of the alphabet with both upper and lowercase letters and pictures, paint the letters of the alphabet in sequence along fencing or walls and draw alphabet snakes on the floor. In addition, display plenty of weatherproof labels, signs and posters. Draw the children's attention to print all over the outdoor environment and plan games and activities that involve physically interacting with and exploring the letters of the alphabet.

Activity 1: What does that say?

Type of activity: Adult-led, small groups.

Resources: Adult supervision for an off-site walk.

What to do: Go out for a walk and look for print in the local environment, for example, signs, posters, maps, road signs, bus/train timetables, menus and price lists. Pause to read them out loud and explain what they mean and what they are used for. Point out different fonts, colours and upper/lower case letters used for emphasis, for instance, to highlight danger or advertise something. Look at the difference between handwritten text on chalkboard menus outside cafés and printed text on shop signs, for example. Discuss which is easier to read.

Key vocabulary: Print, text, writing, sign, advert, poster, read, font, capital, colour, size.

Extension ideas: Ask more able children if they can read any of the signs or posters that you come across.

Look for print in the local environment.

Activity 2: Sort them out

Type of activity: Adult-initiated, during independent play.

Resources: Playground chalks, large tarmacked or slabbed space.

What to do: Draw small circles all over the floor with bright playground chalk and fill them with letters of the alphabet and numbers to 20.

Provide two different light coloured chalks for the children to colour letters in one colour and numbers in another.

Key vocabulary: Letter, number, alphabet, sort, which is which?

Extension ideas: Walk around with the children, point to the circles and ask them if they can identify the letters and numbers.

Activity 3: Alphabet tree

Type of activity: Adult-led, during independent play.

Resources: Mirror letters or colourful wooden letters on string.

What to do: Hang letters on low down branches of trees and bushes around the outdoor area. Call out letter names and see if the children can identify and pick the correct letters from the trees.

Key vocabulary: Letter, find, pick, choose.

Extension ideas: Ask more able children to call out letter names and check if their friends have picked the correct letters.

HOME LINKS

Ask parents to help their children recognise print in the local environment, for example, on road signs, restaurant menus, bus tickets and posters. Suggest they source posters of their children's favourite books or films to display in their bedrooms.

Play games that get children distinguishing between letters and numbers.

Send the children on an alphabet hunt.

Activity 4: Daily notices

Type of activity: Adult-initiated.

Resources: Easel with flip-chart or whiteboard, marker or whiteboard pens.

What to do: Set up an easel in the outdoor area to display daily notices for the children. These could include the weather report, messages and announcements or snack for the day. Draw pictorial symbols alongside the text to help the children decipher what it says.

Key vocabulary: Notice board, daily notices, read, text, writing, what does it say today?

Extension ideas: Set up a smaller blank easel alongside for the children to write their own notices and messages.

Activity 5: Alphabet hunt

Type of activity: Adult-initiated, during independent play.

Resources: Large wooden or plastic letters or alphabet stones, playground chalks or alphabet chart or strip.

What to do: Lay out an alphabet chart or strip, or draw an alphabet strip on the floor using playground chalks. Hide letters all around the outdoor environment and challenge the children to find them all. Explain that they should place each letter they find on the alphabet strip. This will encourage them to match letters, but also help them to figure out which letters are still to be found.

Key vocabulary: Alphabet, letter, find, search, look, match, missing, where?

Extension ideas: Challenge the children to search for objects and place them on the correct initial letter sound on the alphabet strip.

Don't forget to think about...

...teaching children the names of the letters. Children need to know the name of each letter as well as the sound each letter makes.

Activity 6: Twig letters

Type of activity: Adult-initiated, during independent play.

Resources: Baskets of small twigs, laminated alphabet and name cards.

What to do: Set out some baskets of twigs and challenge the children to use them to make the shape of the initial letter in their name.

Give out alphabet cards or draw letter shapes on the floor with playground chalk to help those children who are finding the task a bit tricky.

Key vocabulary: Twigs, letter, shape, form, arrange.

Extension ideas: Challenge more able children to make their full name.

Use sticks to make letters.

HOME LINKS

Set a homework task asking parents to help their children spot and photograph print in the outdoor environment when they are out and about, and send the pictures in to share with the other children in the group.

Enhancing continuous provision

Many early years settings will have a print rich indoor environment with interactive displays, signs and labelling across all areas of learning. However, it is just as important to incorporate print into outdoor provision to bring it to the attention of those more active children who spend most of their time outside.

The following are some suggestions for how to incorporate print into a wide range of outdoor play and activities.

Area of provision	Enhancements that make children aware of print
Water	Drop gel letters into the water tray and provide fishing nets to fish them out. Paint letters on the bottom of boats. Empty the water, replace it with shaving foam and sprinkle letter sequin confetti over the top.
Sand	Bury letters in fine, dry sand and provide spades, rakes and sieves for the children to dig them out. Provide letter shaped sand moulds to use in damp sand. Paint letters on shells and pebbles.
Construction	Provide alphabet blocks for the children to build with, order or arrange into words. Point out and say the letter names.
Role Play	Print off and laminate real examples of environmental print, or set up easels and black boards with handwritten notices and signs to enhance outdoor role-play settings: Shop/market signs (sale, open, closed, reduced, till, customer services, please pay here); door notices (exit, emergency exit, pull, push, toilet); café/restaurant signs (specials, desserts, mains, starters, snacks, hot drinks, cold drinks, self service, menu); construction site signs (roadworks, danger, hard hat area, authorised personnel only); road signs (stop, one way, no entry, give way, no parking, bus stop).
Investigation	Erect a washing line and provide laminated alphabet cards and pegs for the children to hang in sequence or compose words. Provide a basket of alphabet pebbles and challenge the children to find the letters forming their names. Scatter letter sequin confetti around the outdoor area and provide magnifiers for children to look for it.
Physical	Lay out alphabet stepping stones for the children to jump across and balance on. Place a set of alphabet mats on a table and provide clay for children to mould letter shapes.
Garden	Stick laminated alphabet labels on lollypop sticks and push them into the soil around the garden area. Grow cress letters.

Curriculum links

Becoming aware of print covers the following areas of learning and development:

EYFS	Shows interest in illustrations and print in books and print in the environment; recognises familiar words and signs such as own name and advertising logos; knows information can be relayed in the form of print; knows that print carries meaning and in English is read from left to right and top to bottom; names the letters of the alphabet (L).
NIC	Develops concepts of print; understands the purpose and use of environmental print; distinguishes between drawing and writing; understands that writing is a means of communication and can be used for different purposes (LL).
SCE	Explores letters and words, discovering how they work together, and uses what they learn to help them read and write (LE).
WFPF	Understands that written symbols have sound and meaning; experiences and responds to a wide range of print and fonts; understands the connections and differences between: print and pictures; recognises the alphabetic nature of writing and discriminates between letters; understands the different purposes and function of written language as a means of: remembering, organising, developing ideas and information, and as a source of enjoyment (LLC).

Developing phonemic awareness

Once children have had plenty of experience listening to and developing their spoken language, and have a good understanding of the purpose of print, they can be introduced to phonics. In the beginning it is important to concentrate on developing phonemic awareness, or in other words, discriminating between individual sounds in words (phonemes). This means identifying the initial and end sounds as well as sounding out short regular words.

Developing phonemic awareness involves the following skills and concepts:

- Understanding that words can be broken into sounds (phonemes)

- Being able to hear and say the 44 phonemes in the English language

- Being able to identify and say the initial and end sounds in words

- Being able to segment and blend short regular words

- Being able to identify, copy and compose an alliterative phrase.

The following are some ideas for outdoor games and activities that will build children's phonemic awareness. These involve practising listening for and identifying, as well as segmenting and blending sounds in words, which will help children with letter-sound correspondence when they learn to read and write later on.

Activity 1: Sound search

Type of activity: Adult-led, small groups.

Resources: None.

What to do: Send the children to find different objects that begin with a particular sound. When each child returns with their object, ask them to say what it is and identify the initial sound. Then ask them if they can think of another word that begins with the same sound. If they cannot think of anything then offer them some suggestions and give them a chance to have another go.

Key vocabulary: Object, find, search, name, say, word, sound, listen, hear, first, initial.

Extension ideas: Ask more able children to identify the end sound in each word.

Challenge the children to find objects beginning with particular sounds.

Activity 3: Making mistakes

Type of activity: Adult-led, small groups.

Resources: Ebenezer Growmore puppet from page 33.

What to do: Tell the children that although Ebenezer is a very accomplished gardening expert, he finds literacy difficult, and so you thought it might be nice for the children to help him out in return for all the help he gives them in the garden.

Explain that you are going to take Ebenezer around the garden and point out and name lots of different objects. His task is to say the initial sound in each word. It is likely that he will make some mistakes, so the children should listen carefully and help him when he gets them incorrect.

Key vocabulary: Object, name, say, word, sound, listen, hear, first, initial, help, right, wrong, mistake, correct.

Extension ideas: Move on to end sounds. Help Ebenezer segment and blend simple regular words.

HOME LINKS

Encourage parents to support their children's growing knowledge of phonics by suggesting they play some games. Provide examples such as thinking of as many words as they can beginning with the same sound, singing tongue twisting rhymes and making up silly alliterative names for each other.

Activity 2: Name play

Type of activity: Adult-initiated, during independent play.

Resources: Puppet theatre, animal puppets.

What to do: Set up a puppet theatre with a range of animal puppets. As the children are playing ask them if they can think of some names for the puppets based around the initial sound of each animal. For example, Freddie Fox, Bertie Badger and George Giraffe.

Can the children match animals with the same initial sounds? For example, bear, badger and bunny or fox, frog and fish.

Key vocabulary: Name, sound, first, initial, same, hear, say, listen.

Extension ideas: Challenge the children to think of descriptive words for each puppet character that have the same initial sounds. For example, Fun Freddie Fox, Bossy Bertie Badger and Giant George Giraffe. Can they think of foods that match the same sound again? For example, Fun Freddie Fox likes fish fingers or Bossy Bertie Badger likes big burgers.

Sound out action words for the children to follow.

Activity 4: Move it!

Type of activity: Adult-led, small groups.

Resources: Open space, whistle or bells.

What to do: Explain you are going to sound out some movement instructions. The children must listen carefully and follow the instructions. For example, r/u/n, s/t/o/p, h/o/p, j/u/m/p, s/k/i/p, s/i/t, c/l/a/p. Use a whistle or bells as a signal to stop the children each time so they are ready to listen carefully to the next instruction. Begin by both segmenting and blending each word for the children, for example, 's/k/i/p… skip'. Then after a few gos just segment the word and allow the children to blend it themselves.

Key vocabulary: Listen, instruction, move, sound out, segment, blend, sounds, words, stop.

Extension ideas: Choose more able children to sound out instructions to the others.

Activity 5: Tongue twisters

Type of activity: Adult-initiated, during independent play.

Resources: Selection of tongue twisters.

What to do: Join the children as they play and introduce them to some simple alliterative tongue twisters. Try the following:

Whether the weather is warm, whether the weather is hot, we have to put up with the weather, whether we like it or not.

The big bug bit the little beetle, so the little beetle bit the big bug back.

The blue bluebird blinks.

She sells sea shells by the sea shore.

Ensure that you explain to the children that tongue twisters are meant to be difficult to recite, especially quickly.

Key vocabulary: Tongue twister, alliteration, sound, same, first, initial.

Extension ideas: Ask the children to think of alliterative phrases to describe things around them, for example, messy, mucky mud or tough, tall trees. Can they think of alliterative phrases that stem from their names? For example, happy, helpful Harry or lovely, lively Laura.

Don't forget to think about…

…ensuring you model the use of 'pure' sounds. This means pronouncing /m/ as 'mmm' and /t/ as 't', rather than 'muh' and 'tuh'. If children are used to hearing and using pure sounds from the beginning it will be much easier for them to segment and blend the sounds in words accurately.

Activity 6: Sound it out

Type of activity: Adult-led, small groups.

Resources: Computer, printer, laminator, hole punch, string, three-phoneme word picture cards.

What to do: Either use picture cards or source some pictures from the internet, print and laminate them. Focus on three-phoneme words such as c/a/t, m/u/g, sh/ee/p, f/i/sh, b/a/g, b/a/th. Punch holes into the cards, thread with string and hang them all around the outdoor area. Send the children off to find a card. When they return ask them to say what is on the card. Challenge them to segment the word and identify the initial and end sounds.

Key vocabulary: Find, say, sound out, segment, word, sounds, first, initial, end, last.

Extension ideas: Challenge the children to identify the medial (middle) sound in each word. Introduce four-phoneme words.

Enhancing continuous provision

In order to develop phonemic awareness, children need plenty of interactive activities with the support of an adult. Therefore, plan to enhance the learning environment with this in mind, and ensure that practitioners are on hand to join and support the children as they play. Remember that initially the aim is to build children's phonemic awareness rather than linking sounds and letters. Therefore, activities should involve listening and verbal sounding out rather than visual matching.

The following are some ideas for how practitioners can help children become aware of sounds in words during play. Some activities are specifically designed to develop phonemic awareness. However, there are also suggestions for how to incorporate learning about phonemes into everyday play.

Area of provision	Enhancements that help children to develop phonemic awareness
Water	Drop a selection of three-phoneme objects in the water and provide fishing nets. Challenge the children to fish out objects beginning and ending with certain sounds. Can the children segment the entire words? Turn the water tray into a dinosaur swamp. Challenge the children to make up alliterative names for the different dinosaurs, for example, Debbie Diplodocus, George Giganotosaurus or Verity Velociraptor.
Sand	Bury a treasure chest full of three-phoneme objects. Challenge the children to name each object in the chest and segment the sounds. Exchange each object they sound out correctly for a gold coin. Bury a set of objects that all start with the same sound in the sand. Choose a different sound each day and ask the children to dig the objects up and tell you what sound it is.
Construction	Set out the small and large wooden blocks along with a range of large vehicles including tractors, fire engines, diggers, rubbish trucks, cranes, dumper trucks, transporters, bulldozers and lorries. Place a copy of *Dig Dig Digging* by Margaret Mayo and Alex Ayliffe nearby to read with the children. Emphasise the alliterative phrases throughout the book. Play with the vehicles and blocks and use alliterative phrases to describe movements and sounds. Try words like clunk, clang, crash, crumble, crush, tip, tumble, tall, topple, pull, plough, push, pack, drive, drill, drum, grip, grumble, grab, grasp.
Role Play	Witches kitchen: Provide a large cauldron or black bucket, wooden spoons, pots and pans. Challenge the children to find natural ingredients from around the outdoor area that begin with certain sounds to make a potion. Help them to make up alliterative or rhyming spells, for example, Ziggerdy, zaggerdy, zoom or Izzy whizzy let's get busy.
Investigation	Fill a bucket with objects beginning with two different sounds. Place two large hoops next to the bucket and challenge the children to sort the objects according to their initial sounds. Use the same bucket to play a game: the practitioner selects an object and says what it is, then challenges a child to pick out another object that begins with the same sound.
Physical	Provide animal masks and costumes. Join the children as they play, take on the roles of different animals and make different movements while offering alliterative descriptions, for example, slithery slidey snakes, leaping lolloping leopards, cheeky chattering chimps, plump pompous pigs and shy shuffling sheep.
Garden	Set up a small world farm with two, three and four-phoneme animals and objects, such as, p/i/g, sh/ee/p, c/ow, d/o/g, c/a/t, d/u/ck, b/u/ll, g/oa/t, ch/i/ck, sh/e/d, p/o/n/d, v/a/n. Ask the children to pick out animals/objects beginning with certain sounds. While playing, model blending the sounds in each word, for example, Look the d-u-ck… duck is on the pond. Can the children segment any words?

Curriculum links

Developing phonemic awareness covers the following areas of learning and development:

EYFS	Shows awareness of alliteration; hears and says the initial sound in words (L); can segment the sounds in simple words and blend them together (L).
NIC	Identifies and manipulates phonemes; understands that words are made up of sounds; develops auditory discrimination and memory (LL).
SCE	Explores sounds, letters and words, discovering how they work together (LE).
WFPF	Develops phonological knowledge (LLC).

Linking sounds and letters

Once children are aware that words can be broken into sounds, they will be ready to match sounds to letters. There are approximately 44 sounds in the English language and these consist of single letter sounds (phonemes), sounds made of two letters (digraphs) and three letter sounds (trigraphs), although the term 'phoneme' is often used to cover all three. The written representation of a sound is called a grapheme. Children need to be able to confidently match phonemes to graphemes in order to read and write phonetically regular words.

Linking sounds and letters involves the following skills and concepts:

● Understanding that sounds can be represented by one letter (phoneme), two letters (digraph) or three letters (trigraph)

● Understanding that words can be broken into units of sound (phonemes)

● Being able to hear and say the 44 sounds in the English language

● Being able to recognise the written representation of a phoneme (grapheme)

● Being able to match sounds to letters (phonemes to graphemes)

● Being able to segment and blend short regular words.

Use the outdoor environment to inject a bit of fun into phonics.

Activity 1: Letter hunt

Type of activity: Adult-initiated, during independent play.

Resources: Plastic letters, alphabet pebbles, synthetic phonics stones or wooden letter discs.

What to do: Tell the children that there are letters hidden all around the outdoor area and explain that you would like them to go on a letter hunt, bring back as many as they can find and then make as many words as they can out of the letters.

Key vocabulary: Hunt, search, find, letters, sound, blend, words.

Extension ideas: Hide digraph and trigraph wood discs or pebbles to challenge more able children.

Set up an outdoor sound of the week display.

Activity 2: Outdoor sound of the week display

Type of activity: Adult-initiated, during independent play.

Resources: Table, alphabet pebbles, mirror letters, wooden alphabet discs.

What to do: Set up a sound of the week display outdoors to complement the one indoors. Find a sheltered spot to put a table and on it place some alphabet objects featuring the target letter sound, such as alphabet pebbles or wooden discs. Place a few outdoor objects that begin with the target sound on the table, for example, stones, string and snail shells. Draw the children's attention to the table and ask them if they can find anything else to add throughout the week.

Key vocabulary: Letter, sound, display, object, starts with, initial, first, listen, hear, say.

Extension ideas: Bring children to the display regularly to look at the different things that have been contributed.

Activity 3: Sound book

Type of activity: Adult-led, small groups.

Resources: Digital camera, computer, printer, laminator, comb binder.

What to do: Take the children on a walk around a woodland trail or local area. Pause every so often and ask them if they can spot anything that begins with a particular sound. Take photos of the objects they point out.

On returning to the setting, make a sound book with the photos. Each page should feature the letter in the middle surrounded by photos of the objects spotted on the walk. Use the book as an addition to your sound of the week display or put it in the book corner for the children to flick through.

Key vocabulary: Look, name, say, word, sound, listen, hear, first, initial.

Extension ideas: Make a word book with children who are able to sound out regular words.

Don't forget to think about...

...Most settings will have adopted a synthetic phonics scheme and use a systematic approach to teaching these early reading skills during everyday phonics sessions. However, it is extremely important to intersperse focused and repetitive phonics teaching with active and hands-on experiences that will enthuse and capture the interest of all.

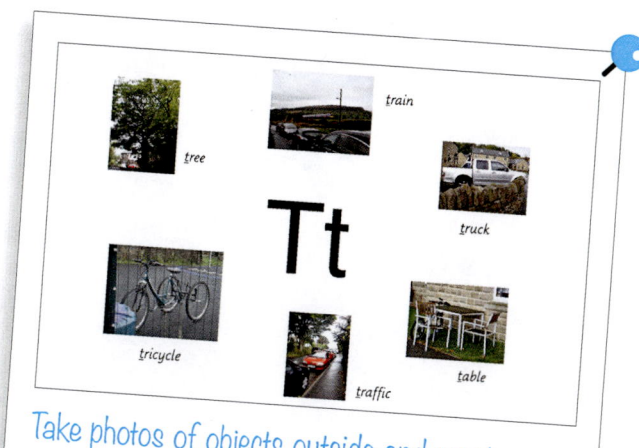

Take photos of objects outside and create a sound book.

Activity 5: Sound aloud

Type of activity: Adult-led, groups of 10.

Resources: 10 cards with letter sounds on them (two of each sound), reasonably large space.

What to do: Give each child a card featuring a letter sound. Explain that someone else in the group has the same letter sound as them. They should look at their card and say the letter sound out loud over and over again, while walking around and listening out to see who else is saying the same sound. When they find their partner they should check their cards look the same, then stand together and wait until everyone else is paired up.

Take in the cards, shuffle them up, hand them out and play the game again.

Key vocabulary: Letter, sound, say, find, listen, match, same.

Extension ideas: Include digraphs and trigraphs to stretch more able children.

Activity 4: Letter dash

Type of activity: Adult-led, groups of up to 10 (to avoid collisions).

Resources: Playground chalks, large space.

What to do: Write six letter sounds on the floor around the edges of a large space.

Gather the children in the middle and explain that you are going to call out a series of words.

The children must listen for the initial sound in each word and run to the correct letter. They are allowed to help each other if they are unsure.

Key vocabulary: Sound, first, initial, listen, run, letter, word.

Extension ideas: Challenge the children to identify and run to end letter sounds. Change the activity into a target game. Provide beanbags and challenge the children to aim for particular sounds.

Activity 6: Fill in the blanks

Type of activity: Adult-initiated, during independent play.

Resources: Playground chalks, large tiles with letters printed on them.

What to do: Draw some large phoneme frames with room for three sounds in each on the floor.

Write in the first and last sound of a word in each frame, leaving the middle sound empty.

Choose initial and end sounds that can be filled with a variety of medial sounds to create different words. For example, s _ t, b _ n, f _ n, r _ n, n _ t and g _ t.

Give the children some large letter tiles and ask them to place them in the middle spaces of the phoneme frames to create words. Get them to sound out the word they have created to see if it makes sense. Challenge the children to move the tiles around to make different words.

Key vocabulary: Words, sounds, letters, initial, first, last, end, middle, make, read.

Extension ideas: Include digraphs such as 'ea', 'oa', 'ee' and 'ai', and the trigraph 'igh' to stretch more able children.

Play games that encourage children to identify middle sounds in words.

Enhancing continuous provision

Again, when learning to link sounds with letters children need plenty of interactive activities with the support of an adult. This means that as well as creating a print rich outdoor environment where children have access to independent phonics activities, it is also important to ensure that practitioners are available to support and assist as well. Many of the suggestions below involve practitioners and children playing together.

Area of provision	Enhancements that help children to link sounds and letters
Water	Drop magnetic letters into the water, provide magnetic fishing rods and ask the children to say the corresponding sound for each letter they catch. Fill letter shaped moulds with coloured water and freeze them. Place these in the water tray for the children to examine, and ask them to say the corresponding sound for each. Set out some buckets with letter sounds stuck to the front. Fill the water tray with slime and drop in objects for the children to fish out and put into buckets that match each object's initial sound.
Sand	Bury alphabet pebbles in the sand and ask children to say the sound for each as they dig them up. Set out some buckets with letter sounds stuck to the front. Bury objects in the sand and provide spades for the children to dig them up and drop them into the buckets that match each object's initial sound.
Construction	Provide wooden alphabet blocks and challenge the children to build short phonetically regular words. Challenge the children to make letter shapes out of blocks. Can other children name the letter and say the sound it makes? Stick regularly spelt name labels on hard hats and high-vis jackets for the children to take on builder roles. Suggestions include, Ben, Nick, Viv, Ted, Jack, Josh, Joan, Dan, Liz and Ella.
Role Play	Market stall: Set up a market stall with sale items arranged by initial letter sound. For example, place baskets of plums, pears and peaches, scones, strawberries and sultanas, and biscuits, beans and bread together. Make large letter labels to display within each section. Make a selection of superhero capes, each featuring a large letter sound so the children can make up their own superhero names to match.
Investigation	Lay out a Bee-bot alphabet mat and challenge the children to program Bee-bot to travel to certain letter sounds. Ask more able children to find initial and end sounds in words and spell out short regular words.
Physical	Set up a table and provide aprons and clay for the children to make into letter shapes. Challenge them to make their names and phonetically regular words out of clay.
Garden	Make large flower heads with coloured paper, laminate them and stick them to short dowel rods. On each flower write on the petals letter sounds that can be used to create words. For example, s, a, t, p, i, n can be used to make tap, sit, pin, sat, nip, tin and sap. Stick the flowers in flower beds and plant pots all over the outdoor area. Challenge the children to pick a flower and make as many words as they can with the letter sounds on its petals.

Curriculum links

Linking sounds and letters covers the following areas of learning and development:

EYFS	Can segment the sounds in simple words and blend them together and knows which letters represent some of them; links sounds to letters; uses phonic knowledge to decode regular words and read them aloud accurately (L).
NIC	Uses word structure to develop reading; identifies and manipulates phonemes; develops visual discrimination and memory; understands that words are made up of sounds and syllables and that sounds are represented by letters (phoneme/grapheme awareness) (LL).
SCE	Explores sounds, letters and words, discovering how they work together, and can use what they learn to help them as they read (LE).
WFPF	Understands that written symbols have sound and meaning and develops phonological knowledge; reads with increasing fluency and accuracy (LLC).

Recognising sight words

Of course for children, learning to read is not as simple as learning '44 phonemes' and blending them. The English language is full of irregularities with many exceptions to the various spelling rules. Young children have the difficult task of gradually learning these rules and exceptions over time. However, to give them an initial boost practitioners can help them to recognise the most commonly occurring irregularly spelt words by sight. In this section there are some suggestions for activities and games that will help children to commit these 'sight words' to memory.

Recognising sight words involves the following skills and concepts:

- Being able to recognise own and friends' names

- Understanding that not all words can be sounded out

- Being able to memorise common sight words

- Being able to identify and read common sight words within a sentence.

One problem with teaching children sight words is that although they may be able to read a word on a flash card or word wall, they sometimes fail to recognise it within a sentence. Therefore, it helps to plan activities and games that put sight words into context and give children strategies for remembering them. The following activities aim to repeatedly expose children to sight words so that they memorise them over time in a playful and active way. There are also suggestions for extending some activities so that children read sight words in context.

Activity 1: Sight word water balloons

Type of activity: Adult-led, during independent play.

Resources: Water balloons, marker pen, playground chalks, large tub.

What to do: Draw a line on the floor with playground chalks. Write sight words in circles on the floor beyond but within throwing distance of the line. Fill some water balloons and write matching sight words on them. Load them into a large tub and invite children to pick them out, read them and throw them at the matching word on the floor.

Key vocabulary: Sight word, read, throw, match, same.

Extension ideas: Use different coloured balloons and arrange children in coloured teams. This will enable you to differentiate the game so that certain teams pick out certain words. Ask the children to put the words into spoken sentences.

Use the outdoor area to make learning sight words fun.

HOME LINKS

Help parents make learning tricky sight words fun with their children at home. Give them a list of ideas, including hiding sight words in surprising places, writing them in chalk on the floor and walls, and writing them on ping-pong balls to play games with.

Activity 2: Bouncy ball

Type of activity: Adult-led, small groups.

Resources: Large, lightweight bouncy ball, different coloured marker pens.

What to do: Write sight words all over a large bouncy ball with different coloured marker pens so that they are easy to distinguish from one another. Ask the children to join hands and form a circle. Explain that the children should bounce the ball to each other. Each time a child receives the ball they should point to a sight word and read it out loud. They are allowed to ask a friend if they need help.

Key vocabulary: Ball, bounce, read, sight word.

Extension ideas: Write sight words in playground chalk all over the floor. Each time a child reads out a sight word from the ball everyone should split off and find the same word on the floor.

Activity 3: Word detectives

Type of activity: Adult-initiated, during independent play.

Resources: Laminated sight word cards or words written on stones or pebbles, playground chalks, magnifying glasses.

What to do: Hide sight word cards all over the outdoor area. Write some short simple sentences on the floor in playground chalk but leave blanks where some sight words should be. Explain the sentences make up clues and the children are the detectives who should solve the puzzle. Give them magnifying glasses and send them off to hunt for the words. They should bring the words back, place them in the sentences, then read the sentences to check the words have been placed correctly and they make sense.

Key vocabulary: Sentence, missing words, find, sight words, fill in, read, make sense.

Extension ideas: Make the sentences longer with trickier words for more able children.

Send the children out on a sight word hunt.

Make a game out of learning sight words.

Activity 4: Giant dominoes

Type of activity: Adult-initiated, during independent play.

Resources: Coloured A4 card, laminator, marker pens.

What to do: Make some giant sight word dominoes to use outdoors. Print or write the words on pieces of A4 coloured card and laminate them. Help the children divide the dominoes between them then take turns to place them. Each time a child places a domino, ensure they pause to read the word before the next child takes their turn.

Key vocabulary: Dominoes, sight words, match, same, read.

Extension ideas: Play the game so that each time a child reads the word correctly they get another turn. If they cannot read the word the next player can try and get a bonus turn if they get it correct. Differentiate the domino sets so that some feature trickier words than others.

Activity 5: Sight word relay

Type of activity: Adult-led, team game.

Resources: Playground chalks, beanbags, marker pens, buckets, large space.

What to do: This is a relay race so needs two or three teams of four to six children. Depending on the number of children and how many are in each team, draw two or three grids with four to six boxes on the floor at one end of a large space. Fill the grids with sight words. Write matching sight words on beanbags with marker pens. Place two or three buckets at the other end of the space and fill these with the corresponding beanbags to match the words on the grids.

Line up each team of children next to a grid. Explain that they should run one at a time to their bucket, grab a beanbag, bring it back and drop it on the matching word on the grid. The team should then read the word before their next runner can take off and get another beanbag from the bucket. The first team to fill their grid wins.

Key vocabulary: Relay race, sight words, match, same, read.

Extension ideas: Get the teams to swap grids and play the game again so they can match and read different words. Differentiate the grids so that some teams have trickier words than others.

Activity 6: Back to back

Type of activity: Adult-led, groups of 10.

Resources: Paper, pen, sellotape.

What to do: Write five sight words on ten pieces of paper (so that there are two of each word). Sellotape the words to the backs of the children. Explain that the aim of the game is for the children to find out what their words are and then find the other child with the same word. They can only do this by helping each other find out what words they have written on their backs. Swap the words around and play the game again. Introduce new words after a few gos.

Key vocabulary: Sight word, read, tell, help, find, same, match.

Extension ideas: Increase the size of the group. Add some trickier words into the mix.

Try...

...creating a permanent word wall in the outdoor area and use it to play games involving searching for and finding particular words, or picking out words that begin with certain letters. Give the children chalks so that they can colour in bricks containing words they know, and include blank bricks on the wall for them to add more. Find a list of 100 high frequency words online (www.highfrequencywords.org).

Enhancing continuous provision

Children gradually commit sight words to memory through frequent exposure to them. As the focused activities on the previous page show, it is possible to do this in a fun way.

Support focused work by enhancing the continuous outdoor provision with a variety of games that make the children familiar with sight words during independent play. Try the following:

Area of provision	Enhancements that help children to recognise sight words
Water	Write sight words on ping-pong balls, float them on the water and provide nets for the children to fish them out. Either call out words for the children to fish out or provide labelled cups for them to drop the matching balls into.
Sand	Print off and laminate some sight words. Stick them to the bottom of a tuff spot with sticky-backed plastic. Pour over a thin layer of fine dry sand and provide small brushes for the children to uncover the words.
Construction	Create a set of word blocks by writing a mixture of phonetically regular and sight words on the sides of building bricks for the children to build their own sentences. When setting up a small world building site, write simple sentences on the floor in playground chalks so that the children can see and read sight words in context. For example: These are big rocks, A tall stack of bricks, The digger is digging up the road.
Role Play	Sight word mine: Set up a dark cave by draping some very thick fabric or black out material over a frame or table. Print off some sight words on white paper and laminate them. Attach them to the inside walls of the cave using sticky-backed Velcro. Write sight words on stones and pebbles and pile them on the floor of the cave. Provide hard hats, high-vis jackets, toy hammers, chisels and drills and give the children torches to go in and mine for the words.
Investigation	Sight word bingo: Draw out bingo boards on the floor with playground chalk and fill them with sight words. Stick matching words onto some giant dice (one die for each board). The children should take turns to roll their dice, read the word and cover the matching word on the board with a beanbag. The first child to cover their board is the winner. Fill a tray with shaving foam and mix in some foam letters. Write some sight words on the floor in playground chalk next to the tray. Challenge the children to find the letters, build the words and read them.
Physical	Use playground chalks to draw giant sight words in joined up writing on the floor. Get the children to trace the words by walking over the letters to help memorise the shape and form of each word. Use playground chalks to draw out a sight word hopscotch. Draw circles on a wall in chalk and fill them with sight words. Provide water squirters and challenge the children to squirt certain words. Tie sight words to the climbing frame. Provide hard hats and rucksacks and send children up to retrieve them.
Garden	Sight word of the day: Print sets of sight words on pebbles, stones, bricks, conkers, laminated paper leaves, flowers and minibeast pictures. Each day choose a sight word and hide items all over the garden that show that particular word. Challenge the children to find all the words each day and drop them in a plant pot or bucket. Hang laminated sight word leaves in trees for the children to spot and read.

Curriculum links

Recognising sight words covers the following areas of learning and development:

EYFS	Recognises familiar words such as own name; reads some common irregular words (L).
NIC	Develops visual discrimination and memory; reads on sight some words in a range of meaningful contexts (LL).
SCE	Explores sounds, letters and words, discovering how they work together, and can use what they learn to help them read (LE).
WFPF	Understands that written symbols have sound and meaning and develops word recognition and contextual understanding; reads with increasing fluency and accuracy (LLC).

Reading

Successful reading involves more than phonics and sight word recognition. It is also important to encourage children to use other reading strategies including using context as a clue to meaning. This can be achieved by planning activities that involve reading for a purpose. Asking children to make sense of a piece of text with the aim of achieving a goal provides context and helps them to make an informed guess when faced with words they cannot read.

Reading involves the following skills and concepts:

- Understanding the purpose of print and recognising the benefits of being able to read

- Being able to blend short regular words

- Being able to identify and read common sight words

- Understanding that in English print is read from left to right and top to bottom

- Being able to guess what a word is, based on the context of the sentence

- Being able to make sense of a piece of text and understand its meaning

- Being able to use pictures as clues.

Use the outdoor area to give reading purpose and context. Plan games and activities that involve reading clues or instructions, include pictures on labels and lists to encourage children to refer to pictures as clues, and make play resources that incorporate meaningful text to encourage children to read as they play.

Activity 1: Easter egg trail

Type of activity: Adult-led, small groups.

Resources: White card, laminator, computer, printer, colouring pencils or pens, glue, scissors, chocolate eggs.

What to do: Set up an Easter egg hunt with written clues to demonstrate the benefits of being able to read. Either find some simple egg designs online and print them out, or draw some and colour them in. Write a series of simple clues that lead on from each other and stick these on the back of the eggs and hide them around the outdoor area.

Accompany the children in small groups and help them read and follow the clues to the end of the trail to find a chocolate prize.

Key vocabulary: Easter, egg, trail, clue, writing, text, read, follow, find.

Extension ideas: Write the clues so that more able children can sound out the words and read them independently.

Look in the shed.

Give children a reason to read.

Activity 2: Scavenger hunt

Type of activity: Adult-initiated, during independent play.

Resources: Descriptive list of items, clipboards, pencils, large containers.

What to do: Write a list of items that can be found in your outdoor area. Ensure that the list is composed of simple descriptions that contain regularly spelt words, sight words and some trickier words that can be read in context. For example, a brown leaf, a round blue ball, a Mobilo wheel, some gravel, a snail shell, a yellow flower, a big round hoop.

Organise scavenger hunts for interested children and set out some large containers. Give them the option to work in teams if they would like. Explain that they should read the list, collect the items and put them in their containers. At the end of the session you will check each team's container against their list to see how many items they found.

Key vocabulary: Scavenger hunt, list, search, find, collect, read, sound out, guess, meaning.

Extension ideas: Differentiate the lists so they have picture clues for less confident readers, and longer descriptions with trickier words for more able readers.

Activity 3: Game on

Type of activity: Adult-initiated, during independent play.

Resources: Large tarmacked or slabbed area, playground chalk, large dice, beanbags (or something to use as counters).

What to do: Draw out a giant game board on the floor. Mark out individual spaces in leaf or flower shapes. Write a number in each shape but every now and again fill a shape with a written instruction, for example, miss a go, roll again, jump forward two spaces, go back three spaces.

Provide a large dice and some counters and show the children how to play. Each time a child lands on an instruction, encourage and help them to read it out loud.

Key vocabulary: Game, dice, roll, move, spaces, how many? read, instruction, miss a go, roll again, move forward, go back, first, winner.

Extension ideas: Compile a set of large laminated cards with simple tasks such as jump three times, hop on the spot, roll down the slope, and lie on your back. Draw out a track with two different coloured spaces. Each time the children land on a particular colour they should pick a card, read it and do the task.

HOME LINKS

Give children research projects to undertake with their parents. Choose a relevant topic or theme and ask parents to take their children to a local library to find out three key pieces of information.

Make play resources that incorporate meaningful text.

Activity 5: Research trip

Type of activity: Whole group visit.

Resources: Transport and adult supervision for a trip off-site.

What to do: Choose a theme or topic of interest that the children are currently preoccupied with.

Gather the children together to talk about it and find out what they know. Ask them if there is anything else they would like to know and if they have any suggestions about how they can find out more.

Explain that they can use information books to learn more, however there are only a few books about this subject at the setting. Ask the children if they know where they might be able to find more books.

Take a trip to a local library to find more books and research the topic further. Spend time looking at the book covers, read the blurb on the back and show the children where the contents and index pages are. Look at the features of information books including the glossary, photos, captions and text. Compare different layouts and ask the children which books they prefer, which are most helpful and why.

Key vocabulary: Books, library, learn, information, read.

Extension ideas: Ask the children if they know any stories about the subject. Find some stories in the library and invite them to bring some in from home.

Activity 4: There be treasure here

Type of activity: Adult-initiated, during independent play.

Resources: Teabag, shallow tray, white paper, coloured pens.

What to do: Make some authentic looking treasure maps. Soak some pieces of white paper in cold tea for a couple of hours. Remove the paper and let it dry completely then crunch it up, open it back out and tear around the edges. Draw out a different map on each piece of paper. Include plenty of details. Give different places names, label landmarks and place a red X to mark the spot.

Provide role-play pirate costumes and telescopes, and make a pirate ship out of a large cardboard box or hollow blocks. Hide a treasure chest somewhere and leave the maps in a role-play ship for the children to discover and use in their play.

Key vocabulary: Map, label, text, writing, read, direction, place name, country, island, sea, ocean, treasure.

Extension ideas: Make accurate maps of the outdoor area that the children can read and use to find hidden objects.

Tip

Look for books with thick card pages if possible as these will fare better outside.

Show the children how to use information books to find out more.

Enhancing continuous provision

Make reading part of everyday life in the early years setting. Source good quality picture and information books with bright, clear illustrations and photos that will attract children to open them up and have a look inside. Place these within each area of outdoor provision for the children to pick up and browse as they play and explore different topics and themes. Demonstrate the benefits of being able to read by using these books to answer the questions that children ask.

Further encourage the children to read by displaying weather proof signs around the outdoor area and labeling storage containers. Point out and help the children read the print around them.

Area of provision	Enhancements that encourage children to read
Water	Fill the water with toy sea creatures and toy fish. Float some boats on the top and add some large rocks, sand, pebbles and shells. Set out a selection of information and story books about sea life and the oceans. Write a simple message in a bottle and float it in the water tray for the children to discover.
Sand	Bury a dinosaur skeleton and provide excavation tools and brushes. Set out a selection of information and story books about fossils and dinosaurs. Write short, simple messages on small pieces of paper, fold them up and put them inside small boxes. Bury the boxes in the sand tray for the children to dig up.
Construction	Set up a wooden train track and provide boxes of wooden blocks, toy people and animals. Set out a selection of information and story books about trains and train journeys. Draw up some architect plans with text and labelling and leave them with the large building blocks.
Role Play	Mobile hairdresser: Fill a carry case with clean hair brushes, combs, hair nets, curlers, plastic scissors (that do not cut!), mirrors, empty spray bottles, a towel, some laminated pictures of hairstyles and children's magazines for customers to read while they have their hair done. Meals on wheels: Label a set of tupperware containers with different meal names and pictures. Make a menu to match. Provide play money and make a car using a banana box for the children to load the food in the back, drive around and sell meals.
Investigation	Set out a selection of substances in bowls on a table, for example, flour, water, washing up liquid, cornflour, rice, lentils, poster and powder paints. Provide mixing bowls and spoons. Set up an easel and write some simple experiment instructions on it. Write, What happens if you… at the top then list different ideas underneath such as, Mix rice and flour? or Mix lentils and blue paint?
Physical	Write physical movement instructions all over the floor of a large space with playground chalks. For example, Jump ten times, Skip to the door, Hop on one leg, Run on the spot and Roll down the hill. Set out a selection of information books about the human body and keeping fit and healthy.
Garden	Display bird, tree, flower and wildlife recognition charts and labelled pictures on the inside of windows facing out. Provide information and story books about birds, plants and wildlife. Leave information books about gardening and growing in the shed or greenhouse.

Curriculum links

Reading covers the following areas of learning and development:

EYFS	Looks at books independently; handles books carefully; holds books the correct way up and turns pages; enjoys an increasing range of books; knows that information can be retrieved from books; demonstrates understanding when talking with others about what they have read (L).
NIC	Reads with some independence; reads a range of texts; knows how to handle and care for books; understands and uses some language associated with books; selects and uses books for specific purposes; uses a range of reading cues with increasing independence and begins to self-correct (LL).
SCE	Engages with a wide range of texts; enjoys exploring and choosing stories and other texts to read or listen to, and can share likes and dislikes; uses signs, books or other texts to find useful or interesting information and uses this to plan, make choices or learn new things (LE).
WFPF	Shows an interest in books and enjoys their content; looks at books with or without an adult, handling them as a reader; is aware of different types of books; experiences and responds to a wide range of print and fonts that include picture books, poems, stories, information, reference and non-literary texts (LLC).

Developing pre-writing skills

One reason why physical development is identified as a prime area of learning in the EYFS is that young children need good control and coordination to hold a pencil and form letter shapes correctly on paper. Before children can be expected to write they should be given the opportunity to develop a number of physical pre-writing skills. These include strengthening the muscles in their wrists, hands and fingers to enable them to grip and manipulate a pencil, developing hand-eye coordination to be able to control a pencil and practising the movements and shapes that writing involves.

Developing pre-writing skills involves the following skills and concepts:

- Having good hand-eye coordination

- Being able to control large and small movements

- Understanding that in English print is written from left to right and top to bottom

- Knowing the four key handwriting movements (l, c, r and z)

- Being able to hold a pencil using a tripod grip

- Being able to manipulate a pencil to form letter shapes.

Children need to take part in large-scale movement activities that build up their body strength so they can hold the correct posture to sit and write. They also need to develop their hand-eye coordination and muscle tone to be able to hold a pencil, manipulate and control it. Once they have developed these skills they can begin to practise forming letter shapes. Use the following outdoor activities to complement the letter formation practice that is part of daily literacy indoors.

Activity 1: Obstacle course

Type of activity: Adult-initiated, during independent play.

Resources: Climbing frame, slide, benches, hoops, cones, tyres, stepping stones, tunnels, crash mats.

What to do: Set up an obstacle course for the children to tackle and improve their coordination and control. Incorporate a climbing frame if possible for them to practise climbing and balancing. Place benches the right way up as well as upside down to increase the challenge. Use cones, hoops, tyres and stepping stones to create obstacles that need to be stepped over, avoided or weaved around. Place crash mats in places where children are likely to lose their balance.

Key vocabulary: Balance, travel, coordination, control, move, take care, avoid, around, over, through, under.

Extension ideas: Place small items around and about the apparatus, taking care to place them where the children cannot trip over them. Challenge the children to collect these items and place them in a bum bag as they negotiate the course.

Provide interesting opportunities for mark-making.

Activity 3: Sky writing

Type of activity: Adult-led, small groups (try to divide right and left handed children into separate groups).

Resources: Open space.

What to do: Take the children outside and practise the four key handwriting movements by sky writing the letters in each group:

Long ladder group (l): l t l u y j
Curly caterpillar group (c): c a d e g o q f s
One armed-robot group (r): b h k m n p r
Zigzag group (z): v w x z

Focus on one group at a time and begin by getting children to move their arms from their shoulders to create large movements in the air. As they become more confident, encourage them to gradually refine their movements until they are able to draw the letter shapes with a pointed index finger.

Key vocabulary: Letter, form, shape, movement, direction, large, small, control, write.

Extension ideas: Challenge children to write their names in the air.

Activity 2: Upside down

Type of activity: Adult-initiated, during independent play.

Resources: Table, large sheets of paper, tub of pens, pencils and crayons, large blanket, sellotape.

What to do: Make mark-making more exciting while strengthening hand and wrist muscles by setting up an upside down writing den. Sellotape large sheets of paper to the underside of a table and drape a blanket over the top so it covers three sides. Provide a tub of crayons, pens and pencils and invite the children to lie inside on their backs and write on the ceiling.

Key vocabulary: Write, draw, picture, crayon, pen, pencil, den, ceiling.

Extension ideas: Tape pieces of paper on the underside of benches, tables and other outdoor furniture for the children to discover. Provide post-it notes for them to leave secret messages of their own.

Tip

Use sky writing to practise the correct formation of numerals as well. However, to avoid confusion do not practise writing both letters and numerals at the same time.

Help children to improve their coordination and practise directionality through physical activity.

Activity 4: Write direction

Type of activity: Adult-initiated, during independent play.

Resources: Playground chalks, natural objects collected from the outdoor area.

What to do: Use patterns to help children get used to making marks from left to right. Use playground chalks to start some repeating patterns on the floor and challenge the children to continue them. Otherwise, start patterns using natural objects such as conkers, sycamore seeds or leaves. Begin the patterns at the left hand side of window sills, at the top of pathways and at the left hand side of tables or benches to encourage the children to continue them to the right.

Key vocabulary: Pattern, continue, add to, what next, direction, right.

Extension ideas: Invite children to start their own patterns and get their friends to continue them.

Don't forget to think about…

…left handed children. When demonstrating key handwriting movements and letter formation, ensure you give left handed children specific attention and model the movements with your left hand.

Activity 5: Crossing over

Type of activity: Adult-led, whole group.

Resources: Large open space.

What to do: Help children to improve their coordination by practising cross lateral movements. Ask them to spread out and copy your demonstration of the following:

- Bend over and touch your left foot with your right hand, straighten up then bend to touch your right foot with your left hand, and repeat
- Lift your right knee and touch it to your left elbow and vice versa, then repeat
- Reach over and touch your left earlobe with your right hand and vice versa, then repeat
- Stretch your arms out straight in front of you, cross them over, turn your palms to face each other, link your hands and fold your arms in toward your body
- Hold your right arm straight out in front of you, stick your thumb up and move your entire arm from the shoulder in the shape of an eight lying on its side, then repeat with the other arm.

Key vocabulary: Exercise, coordination, control, copy, movement, left, right.

Extension ideas: Give the children ribbon wands and encourage left handed children to make shapes with them in their right hand and vice versa.

Activity 6: Wacky races

Type of activity: Adult-led, small groups.

Resources: Large space, preferably a school field with a racetrack marked out, large spoons, small potatoes, beanbags, large bouncy balls, stilts.

What to do: Help children develop their hand-eye coordination by setting up some wacky races that require them to move while balancing, throwing, bouncing and catching objects. Get them to race while balancing potatoes on spoons or beanbags on heads, bouncing a ball, walking on stilts or throwing and catching a ball or beanbag.

Key vocabulary: Race, throw, catch, bounce, watch, look, balance, go.

Extension ideas: At the end of the racetrack set out some buckets and jumbo tweezers with ten small objects such as wooden cubes or conkers. When the children reach the end they must pick up the objects with the tweezers and drop them in the bucket. The first to do so is the winner.

Enhancing continuous provision

Help children get ready to write by setting up activities that will help them to build the muscle tone in their arms, hands and fingers to prepare them for holding a pencil. Give them toys and equipment that will help them to develop their coordination and gross and fine motor control. Set up games and activities that will encourage them to practise handwriting movements and make letter shapes.

Encourage children to make marks by hanging black boards on outside walls, setting up easels loaded with paints, crayons and pens, and leaving small whiteboards and pens lying around.

Area of provision	Enhancements that help children develop pre-writing skills
Water	Drop sponges in soapy water for children to squeeze. Mix cornflour with water, spread it over the surface of a tuff spot and provide mark making tools. Squeeze and mould snow to make snowballs and snow-people.
Sand	Sprinkle dry sand, rice, couscous, flax seed or quinoa onto a tuff spot and provide brushes and tools for children to make marks and draw. Drop small objects onto the sand and provide tweezers and tongs for the children to pick them out.
Construction	Provide construction toys that require good coordination, careful manipulation and fine motor control such as LEGO, DUPLO, Stickle Bricks, Mobilo, Popoids, Magnetico and Junior Engineer. Give the children playground chalks so they can draw plans and diagrams on the floor.
Role Play	Painters and decorators: Provide overalls, buckets filled with water and large paintbrushes for children to pretend to paint the walls. Laundrette: Provide tubs of soapy water and a scrubbing board for children to wash, scrub and squeeze out clothes. Set up a washing line and supply some pegs for the children to pinch and secure the clothes on the line to dry.
Investigation	Provide a selection of large floor puzzles for children to practise hand-eye coordination. Roll out and weigh down large sheets of black paper on the floor. Fill squeezy bottles with brightly coloured paint for the children to squeeze and squirt patterns. Fill plastic wallets with thick poster paint and seal them. Provide mark making implements such as cotton buds for the children to scrape over the surface and make patterns and marks.
Physical	Provide ribbons for children to manipulate and weave through railings. Set out some large letter stencils with paper and pencils in a tuff spot on the floor. Provide small and large balls and set up nets, goals and targets for the children to develop hand-eye coordination whilst aiming, throwing and catching.
Garden	Place sensory stones imprinted with letter shapes amongst the plants and shrubbery for children to run their fingers over and practise letter formation. Provide watering cans in different sizes and shapes for the children to develop muscle tone and coordination as they fill, aim and pour the water onto plants. Collect a large amount of big leaves and put them on a table with felt pens for the children to trace over the veins.

Curriculum links

Developing pre-writing skills covers the following areas of learning and development:

EYFS	Shows control in holding and using mark-making tools; draws lines and circles using gross motor movements; shows a preference for a dominant hand; holds pencil near point between first two fingers and thumb and uses it with good control; begins to use anti-clockwise movement and retraces vertical lines (PD).
NIC	Shows increased control over formation of lower and upper-case letters (LL). Handles small tools, objects, construction and malleable materials safely and with increasing control (PD).
SCE	Is learning to move body well, exploring how to manage and control it and finding out how to use and share space; is developing movement skills through practise and energetic play (HW).
WFPF	Experiments with mark-making, using a variety of media (LLC). Develops coordination, gross motor skills and fine manipulative skills; controls body movements; develops muscle tone; develops gross and fine motor skills through practical activities and use of varied tools, equipment and apparatus (PD).

Writing

Once children have a secure understanding of the purpose of print, are able to link sounds and letters, and have developed the physical ability to hold and use a pencil, they can begin to learn to write. Writing is a complex task and the challenge should not be underestimated. Children need to think about what they are going to write, form it into a sentence, spell out the words they want to use and form the letters correctly.

Writing involves the following skills and concepts:

- Understanding the purpose of print and recognising the benefits of being able to write

- Understanding that in English, print is written from left to right and top to bottom

- Being able to translate a thought into a sentence

- Knowing the four key handwriting movements (l, c, r and z)

- Being able to hold and use a pencil correctly to write letters

- Being able to segment short regular words

- Being able to read and write common sight words.

Children learn to write through focused guided activities with the help of an adult. However, practitioners can support this learning by using the outdoor area to inspire children to experiment with and practise early writing during play.

Activity 1: Can I take a message?

Type of activity: Outdoor resource set up by an adult.

Resources: Role-play telephone box or large cardboard box and small table, scissors, red paint, PVA glue, notepads, post-it notes, pens, pencils, phone, phone book.

What to do: Set up a role-play telephone box. Either use a commercially produced telephone box or make one using a tall, narrow cardboard box. Cut out a door, paint the box red and coat it in watered down PVA glue. Place a telephone book and phone inside and a small table outside with note taking equipment.

Key vocabulary: Telephone box, phone, ringing, answer, message, write, deliver, tell, pass along, call back.

Extension ideas: Set up a message board. Use an easel and provide markers for children to write each other messages.

Encourage children to write as they play.

Activity 3: Spell it out

Type of activity: Adult-initiated, during independent play.

Resources: Playground chalks, toys and objects, large tarmacked or slabbed space.

What to do: Spread some toys and objects around an open space. Provide a tub of playground chalks and challenge the children to label each object by writing what it is underneath. Choose simple objects that can be phonetically spelt, for example, car, ball, box, mat, cap, sock, bag and doll.

Key vocabulary: Write, spell, sound out, segment, blend, letter, sound, form.

Extension ideas: Include objects that are spelled using digraphs and trigraphs, for example leaf, boat, book, chair and tights to stretch more able children.

Tip

Provide different sized post-it notes for children to write on. Large post-it notes are great for big writing and small post-it notes are good for helping children develop finer motor control as they attempt to write in smaller text.

Activity 2: Daily question

Type of activity: Adult-initiated, on arrival at setting.

Resources: Large white board easel, drywipe pens.

What to do: Stand an easel just outside the entrance to the setting. Each day write a different question at the top and encourage parents to help their children record an answer. Questions could include anything, for example; What did you have for breakfast? How are you feeling today? What is your favourite colour? What is your pet's name?

Try to ensure the question only demands a one or two word answer so that children do not feel overwhelmed, and a traffic jam does not build up at the entrance. Less confident writers can ask parents to write the answers for them, whereas those children who are able to can attempt to write the answers themselves.

Key vocabulary: Question, answer, write.

Extension ideas: Leave whiteboards around the outdoor area with questions that require children to choose between two answers. For example, Do you like pink or blue flowers best? Are you better at riding a tricycle or scooter? Do you like the rain, yes or no? Write the question at the top with answer columns underneath. Children can then write their name under their chosen answer.

Invite the children to set up their own small world scene and 'write' a story to go with it.

Activity 4: Outdoor word bank

Type of activity: Outdoor resource set up by adult.

Resources: Computer, printer, card, guillotine, laminator, sticky backed Velcro.

What to do: Create a word bank inside a shed or playhouse that the children can refer to when they are writing outside. Stick pieces of Velcro on an inside wall and attach laminated key vocabulary cards that the children can remove and use to help them as they write on clipboards, notepads, wall mounted black boards, easels and tables around the outdoor area.

Key vocabulary: Word bank, words, vocabulary, topic, theme, copy, help, write.

Extension ideas: Build up sets of words that link to topics, and change the word bank to reflect changing themes.

Activity 5: Making sense

Type of activity: Adult-initiated, small groups.

Resources: Mole hills, natural objects, digital camera, small world animals, creatures and characters, clipboard, paper and pen.

What to do: Explain that you would like the children to create a story scene by turning mole hills into castles using natural objects. Give the children plenty of time to forage for objects and create their scene.

As the children work, ask them to tell you about the castle they are building and its design. Ask them who lives in the castle. Allow them to choose from a selection of small world characters and creatures (or to create their own) and leave them to play and develop their own storyline.

When the children have had time to play, visit each group with a clipboard and encourage them to narrate a story about their castle and its inhabitants. As they tell the story continually prompt them to put their ideas into complete sentences that make sense. Scribe for them and read it back so they can hear what they have 'written'.

Key vocabulary: Story, begin, start, what happened next? character, name, sentence, does that make sense?

Extension ideas: Create a storyboard by taking photos of the small world scene and pasting these alongside the sentences provided by the children. Encourage more able children to write their own sentences underneath.

Try...

...turning an outdoor shed into a writing den and filling it with paper, pens, pencils, staplers, hole punches, bulldog clips, paper clips, sticky labels, diaries, calendars, files, clipboards and folders.

HOME LINKS

Send a puppet or cuddly toy home with a different child each weekend, with a diary for parents and children to fill in together. Explain that children can draw a picture and parents can add some comments. If children are able to they can write a sentence or two as well.

Challenge the children to create a creature and build a story around it.

Enhancing continuous provision

Help children learn to write by providing literacy materials that they can use to practise segmenting and blending letters to spell words, as well as putting words together to build sentences. Encourage them to make marks and attempt to write by leaving small white boards, chalk boards, clipboards and paper all around the outdoor area that they can pick up, draw and write on whenever they like.

Demonstrate the purpose of writing by modelling the use of writing materials during role-play, when scoring games and designing models.

Area of provision	Enhancements that encourage children to write
Water	Set up an easel with a drywipe white board and pens next to the water tray for the children to record scores, draw diagrams and write notes as they play. Provide plastic bottles, paper and pens for sending messages in bottles.
Sand	Fill a tuff spot with damp compressed sand and provide tools for children to draw and write on the surface. Bury a treasure chest and provide blank tea-stained paper for the children to make their own pirate treasure maps.
Construction	Roll out large pieces of plain paper and provide pens, pencils and rulers for the children to draw and label their own building plans. Fill tool belts with notepads, post-it notes and pencils.
Role Play	Post office: Turn the playhouse or shed into a post office. Make a postbox out of a large cardboard box. Set up a counter inside with trays, envelopes, writing paper, postcards, fake postage stamps, weighing scales, till, computer keyboard, telephone, ink pad and stamp, pens and pencils. Put sticky backed Velcro on ride-on vehicles and laminated blank white cards. Provide drywipe pens for the children to create their own personalised number plates.
Investigation	Set up a white board easel and provide sets of magnetic letters and words for the children to build sentences. Leave mark-making implements next to dried patches of mud for children to write in. Challenge children to find stones that will write on walls.
Physical	Crush up playground chalks and mix them with water to make paints. Provide paintbrushes and whole chalks for the children to draw, paint pictures and write on the floor and walls. Help them to work together to create a large chalk wall mural.
Garden	Provide plant label sticks and pens. Make some blank minibeast fact cards. Print pictures of minibeasts on A4 paper with a large blank space underneath. Laminate these and leave them in the garden with drywipe pens for children to write on.

Curriculum links

Writing covers the following areas of learning and development:

EYFS	Gives meaning to marks they make as they draw, write and paint; can segment the sounds in simple words and blend them together; uses phonic knowledge to write words in ways which match their spoken sounds; writes some common irregular words; writes simple sentences that can be read by themselves and others (L).
NIC	Understands that writing is a means of communication and can be used for different purposes; shares their writing with others; writes without prompting and makes decisions about how and what they will write; begins to problem solve how to write using sound/symbol correspondence as the first strategy; shows increased control over formation of lower and upper-case letters, size and spacing (LL).
SCE	Explores sounds, letters and words, discovering how they work together, and can use what they learn to help as they read or write; as they play and learn, enjoys exploring interesting materials for writing and different ways of recording experiences and feelings, ideas and information (LE).
WFPF	Recognises the alphabetic nature of writing and discriminates between letters; communicates by using symbols, pictures and words; begins to write in a conventional way, communicating by using words, phrases and short sentences, linked to familiar patterns; develops their ability to spell common and familiar words in a recognisable way; develops a legible style of handwriting in order to follow the conventions of written English (LLC).

Planning and organising outdoor literacy

Every setting has a different outdoor environment with particular features and limitations. A large area needs to be designed carefully to ensure the best possible use of space. On the other hand, practitioners with small outdoor areas need to think about how they can make use of nearby public spaces or the possibility of taking regular trips further afield.

When planning and organising outdoor literacy provision, it is important to think about how the outside environment can be utilised to complement and extend the learning that is happening indoors. Outdoor provision is about taking advantage

of the unique characteristics of the outside environment and using them to enhance teaching and learning. Use outdoor space to help children build their strength and develop gross and fine motor skills, use the natural elements to help them improve their speaking, listening and language skills, plan active games that teach them about phonics, and enhance their outdoor play with reading and writing resources.

Plan outdoor learning in the same detail as you would do indoors. Draw a diagram of both the indoor and outdoor areas, including permanent fixtures. Photocopy these and use one for each day of the week. Handwrite planned activities and resources onto the diagrams, ensuring you consider logistics in terms of indoor and outdoor supervision. Take account of where adult-led activities are to be carried out during each session and plan so that adults are occupying both spaces at all times.

If possible, make life easier by setting up early in the morning before the children arrive. Otherwise pass the planning diagram to a support assistant and ask them to set up while the children settle in during the first fifteen minutes of the day.

Literacy in a large outside space

Practitioners who are lucky enough to have a large space should consider providing the following:

- Physical resources that build upper body strength, and improve coordination, including skittles, bats, balls, beanbags, targets, climbing and balancing apparatus

- Big construction equipment for children to build on a large scale

- Dens and shelters for role-play, as well as quiet talking, reading and writing

- Wall mounted chalkboards, easels and playground chalks for children to paint, draw and write

- Large sand and water play equipment for children to develop strength in wrists, arms and hands as they dig, mould and pour

- Stage for performing, singing and dancing.

Literacy in a small outside space

Practitioners who have a smaller space might like to consider providing the following:

- Functional dividers such as large storage containers or planters to make the best possible use of space while sectioning off areas

- Letters painted on fencing panels and alphabet charts painted on the floor

- Themed role-play boxes containing costumes and accessories that can be easily stacked, stored and brought outside

- Small construction toys that develop fine motor control

- Pop-up tents for quiet talking, reading and writing

Use the outdoor environment to set up physical activities that help prepare children for writing later on.

- Wheeled trolleys with stacked baskets for transporting resources between indoor and outside areas

- Mirrored letters and alphabet bunting hanging from trees or shelters

- Sand and water trays to dig, pour and mould on a smaller yet still messy scale

- Handheld whiteboards, chalkboards, clipboards and small easels for children to paint, draw and write.

Don't forget to think about...

...no matter what size the outdoor area is, the children should have free and open access to a range of resources that will help them to independently sustain and develop their play. What's more, the layout should, as far as possible, facilitate physical activity as well as quiet play and conversation.

Collecting evidence of children's learning

The EYFS highlights observation as integral to teaching and learning. It is through observing children that practitioners get a rounded view of their interests, learning needs and attainment levels. The Framework states that learning experiences should be shaped according to observation outcomes. Some children do most of their learning outside, and it is just as important to observe outdoors as it is indoors.

Observing outdoors

Make observation outdoors as logistically possible as it is indoors. Ensure that practitioners have the correct equipment to hand so they can carry out good quality observations when outside:

- Secure wall-mounted slings or wallets just inside the doorway leading out to the outdoor area. Use it to keep clipboards, pens, post-it notes and cameras that practitioners can reach in and grab quickly when the need arises.

- Print off sheets of sticky labels for snap-shot observations. Design a template for each label with headings including, name of observer, date, time, name of child, area of learning and observation. These are quick to fill in and easy to transfer to assessment profiles.

- Fill waterproof bum bags with pens, post-its and digital cameras.

- Ensure that every clipboard has a few plastic sleeves on it to protect notes from rain and messy play.

- Use dictaphones to record children's thoughts and comments as they play. This is more practical during messy physical activities that make holding a clipboard awkward.

Observation should be a fully inclusive process during which practitioners draw information from a variety of sources to gain a rounded view of the child. However, the EYFS acknowledges the burden of too much paperwork and stresses that assessment should not be carried out at the expense of interacting with the children.

Bearing this in mind, the example observation sheet on page 80 is designed to hold a large amount of information on a single document. There is space for recording the observation and assessment notes, as well as comments from other professionals, children and parents.

Observing and assessing literacy learning

When assessing communication, language and literacy skills it is helpful to have a list of assessment questions to refer to. Attach the list to your clipboard to help keep curriculum requirements in mind while observing. The list should help you to consider whether the children are:

- Using auditory discrimination to identify sounds in the environment

- Aware of sounds in language

- Able to concentrate and maintain attention

- Able to form clear speech sounds

- Listening to and responding appropriately to others

- Using a growing vocabulary and expressing themselves clearly

- Demonstrating phonemic awareness

- Recognising sight words

- Attempting to read using a variety of strategies

Ensure practitioners have the correct equipment to hand so taking good quality observations is just as possible outside.

- Engaging in independent mark-making and writing.

When observing an adult-led literacy activity it is helpful to observe with specific learning objectives in mind. There are different ways to do this. Either ensure the objectives are clearly stated in the planning and copy them onto observation sheets, or include an assessment section on planning documents to record observation notes.

Assessing outdoor provision

Assess the use of outdoor space and resources by observing children's movements. This can be done through tracking observations, where practitioners focus on one child at a time and track their movements on a diagram of the outdoor area. The practitioner may either observe a child continuously for 10 minutes, or for five minutes every 15 minutes over the course of an hour. They track the child's movements from one activity to the next and record how long the child remains at each. By choosing to observe a good cross section of children in one session, practitioners can gain a clear picture of how well the outdoor space is working to suit particular needs and purposes.

Tracking observations can also be used to help practitioners assess how well subject-specific resources are working to enhance learning. This involves observing particular spaces and the use of resources instead of focusing on specific children. In the case of literacy, practitioners may choose to observe how well children make use of outdoor reading and writing areas. It might be that the reading area is not inviting or comfortable enough, leading practitioners to invest in some outdoor beanbags or picnic blankets and large cushions. Otherwise, children may be ignoring writing equipment, leading practitioners to consider how they can plan activities that give children a reason to pick up these resources and write.

Don't forget to think about...

...using digital observations to capture snapshots of children's learning. Photographs, film and audio recordings save time and capture a much more rounded picture than hurried handwritten notes.

Literacy observation record

Literacy observation record

Child's name:

Observer's name:

Area of provision/Focused activity:

Specific learning objectives:

Date:

Start time:

End time:

Observation notes:
Record here children's actions, comments and conversation.

Assessment questions:
Consider these questions in relation to the above observation.

Is the child...

Using auditory discrimination to identify sounds in the environment?

Aware of sounds in language?

Able to concentrate and maintain attention?

Able to form clear speech sounds?

Listening to and responding appropriately to others?

Demonstrating phonemic awareness?

Recognising sight words?

Attempting to read using a variety of strategies?

Engaging in independent mark-making and writing?

Using a growing vocabulary and expressing themselves clearly?

Assessment notes:

Implications for future planning:
Note down here any ideas stemming from this observation about investigations, activities or resources that build upon the findings of this observation.

Resources and further reading

Resources

- Magnetic fish and rods, talking tubes, forest phones, squidgy sparkle letters, Junior Engineer construction sets, A4 laminated white boards, coloured drywipe pens (www.reflectionsonlearning.co.uk)

- Wooden alphabet blocks, jumbo chalks, chubby crayons, chunky triangular pencil crayons, easy grip paint brushes (www.elc.co.uk)

- Sound prisms, outdoor clothing, weather resistant alphabet learning boards, large weather resistant chalk boards, alphabet pebbles, wire book racks, Stickle Bricks, Popoids (www.earlyyearsdirect.com)

- Rainbow sound blocks, Easi Speak microphones, tuff spot trays and adjustable stands, magnetic words (www.earlyyearsresources.co.uk)

- Junk music walls and kits, musical guttering, wall xylophone, metal chimes frame, small construction straw bales, mini life size bricks, Bear Hunt waterproof vinyl storyline scene cards, teddy bear wooden party tea set, superhero capes and writing cuffs, flower fairies, fairy garden table, rustic castles, dragons, outdoor library station, reading shed, portable book rack, alphabet stepping stone wooden discs, synthetic phonics stones, digraph/trigraph wood discs, writing belts, alphabet bunting, outdoor cushions and beanbags (www.cosydirect.com)

- Tell me a story sequencing cards, traditional tales wooden characters, fairy fantasy scene kit, wooden superhero characters, mirror letters, jumbo tweezers, feels-write letter stones (www.yellow-door.net)

- Wind chimes, talking-Point recording devices, MP3 recorders, talking clipboards, child-friendly digital cameras, mini mobile phones, walkie talkies, voice changer, friendship stop signs, outdoor puppet theatre, Bee-bot, Bee-bot alphabet mat (www.tts-group.co.uk)

- Carousel CD of nursery rhymes and children's songs; Outdoor Beat Baby by Ros Bayley (www.lawrenceeducational.co.uk)

- Traditional story sets of finger puppets (http://uk.thepuppetcompany.com)

- Small football goals, letter sequin confetti (www.amazon.co.uk) and (www.ebay.co.uk)

Further reading

- *50 Fantastic Ideas for Imaginative Thinking* by Marianne Sargent (Featherstone, 2014)

- *Communication, Language and Literacy from Birth to Five* by Avril Brock and Carolynn Rankin (Sage, 2008)

- *Foundations of Literacy* by Sue Palmer and Ros Bayley (Featherstone, 2013)

- *Let's Take a Story Book Outside* by Ruth Ludlow (Lawrence Educational, 2008)

- *Literacy Outdoors* by Ros Bayley, Helen Bromley and Lynn Broadbent (Lawrence Educational, 2006)

- *Outdoor Learning in the Early Years: Management and Innovation* by Helen Bilton (Routledge, 2010)

- *Outdoor Play* by Sue Durant (Practical Pre-School Books, 2013)

- *Playing with sounds: A supplement to Progression in Phonics* (Department for Education and Skills, 2004) Accessed online: https://public.rgfl.org/PrimaryStrategy/Literacy/Shared%20Documents/Letters%20and%20Sounds/Playing%20with%20sounds.pdf

- *This Little Puffin* by Elizabeth Matterson (Puffin, 1991).

- *The Road to Writing: A step-by-step guide to mark making 3-7* by Sue Cowley (Continuum, 2012)

Useful websites

- Learning Through Landscapes: www.ltl.org.uk

- Write Dance: www.writedancetraining.com

- Creative Star Learning Company: http://creativestarlearning.co.uk/c/literacy-outdoors/

References

Bilton, H. (2010) *Outdoor Learning in the Early Years: Management and Innovation*. Routledge, Oxon.

Bruner, J. (1966) *Toward a Theory of Instruction*. Harvard University Press, Cambridge, MA.

Council for the Curriculum, Examinations and Assessment (CCEA) (2006) Northern Ireland Curricular Guidance for Pre-School Education. CCEA, Belfast.

Council for the Curriculum, Examinations and Assessment (CCEA) (2007) Northern Ireland Curriculum: Primary. CCEA, Belfast.

Department for Children, Education, Lifelong Learning and Skills (DCELLS) (2008) Foundation Phase Framework for Children's Learning for 3 to 7-year-olds in Wales. DCELLS Publications, Cardiff.

Department for Children, Education, Lifelong Learning and Skills (DCELLS) (2008a) Foundation Phase Framework: Learning and Teaching Pedagogy. DCELLS Publications, Cardiff.

Department for Education (DfE) (2014) Statutory Framework for the Early Years Foundation Stage. DfE Publications, Nottingham.

Learning and Teaching Scotland (LTS) (2010) *Curriculum for Excellence through Outdoor Learning*. LTS, Glasgow.

Palmer, S. Bayley, R. and Broadbent, L. (2013) *Foundations of Literacy*. Featherstone, London.

Piaget, J. (1952) *The Origins of Intelligence in Children*. International Universities Press, New York.

Siraj-Blatchford, I., Sylva, K., Muttock, S., Gilden, R., Bell, D. (2002) *Researching Effective Pedagogy in the Early Years [REPEY]: Research Report No 356*. HMSO, London.

Siraj-Blatchford, I., Sylva, K., Melhuish, E., Sammons, P., Taggart, B. (2004) *Effective Provision of Pre-school Education [EPPE] Project: Final Report*. DfES, London and Institute of Education, University of London.

Sylva, K., Melhuish, E., Sammons, P., Siraj, I., Taggart, B., with Smees, R., Toth, K., Welcomme, W., Hollingworth, K. (2014) *Effective Pre-school, Primary and Secondary Education [EPPSE 3-16] Project: Research Report*. University of Oxford; Birbeck, University of London; Institute of Education, University of London.

Tickell, C. (2011) *The Tickell Review: The Early Years: Foundations for life, health and learning*. HMSO, London.

Vygotsky, L. (1986) *Thought and Language*. MIT Press, Cambridge, MA.